When Shovels Break

A candid, true story about discouragement, falling away from our faith, and the possibility of forgiveness.

Michael J. Shank

A man's very highest moment is, I have no doubt at all, when he kneels in the dust and beats his breast, and tells all the sins of his life.

— Oscar Wilde

We can only know God well when we know our own sin. And those who have known God without knowing their wretchedness have not glorified Him but have glorified themselves.

— Blaise Pascal

Thank You

I want to say thank you to Bradley Cobb, Shane Otts, and Glenn Davis. These men are not only my brothers in Christ, but they are dear friends and men who are directly responsible for the success of my first book, *Muscle and a Shovel*.

For Your Eyes Only

This story is *not* intended for the lost, perishing, alien sinner. It is intended *only for New Testament Christians*.

Caution

A story can be a window into the soul, and some stories, like this one, reveal things about us that we want no one to know. They are those deep, dark, hidden thoughts and behaviors that bring shame and destruction to our lives, and the lives around us. Bringing these things into the light brings about our biggest fear: judgment and rejection by those we love the most.

This story will shock you. Regardless of the potential controversy and backlash, this story *must* be told.

You're about to find out why…

They that are whole have no need of the physician, but they that are sick: I came not to call the righteous, but sinners to repentance.

Mark 2:17

Chapter 1
Sweat and a Shotgun
August, 2004: Lake Dallas, Texas

"John, please give me the gun," I said in soft, low
tones. My legs trembled from fear over the stress of what
was happening at that moment. *Dear Father, help me
help him* was the silent prayer racing through my mind.

There we stood in my two-car garage just outside
of Dallas, Texas. I was in boxer shorts and an old
University of Tennessee T-shirt. It was midnight in our
suburban Lake Dallas neighborhood of well-manicured,
upscale, four-thousand square-foot brick homes, all built
closely together right off of I35 North (toward Denton,
Texas) at the Swisher Road exit – Owen Oaks Drive.
Most of the neighbors were asleep for the night.

Why was John at my house again tonight? More
trouble in his life. John's car had just been repossessed
from his driveway a few hours earlier.

John was a lifelong friend. I met him at the age of
thirteen, and he knew me better than anyone. He knew me
better than my *wife* knew me. We were as close as any
two brothers could be. We had stayed together throughout
life, and here he was in Lake Dallas with us again.

But I had a secret about John. The secret? Deep
down in my heart-of-hearts, I hated him. Hated him for
his choices and his behavior. Hated him for all of the

stupid things he'd done over the past fifteen years. Hated him for his failures and sins and all that he had put his family through. Hated him for what he'd done to me and my own family. Hated his foolish weakness. Hated his narcissism, selfishness, and arrogance. Hated him for his sins. And I hated him because he was always around causing problems in our lives.

The irony of our relationship was that John *knew* I hated him, but he simply wouldn't get out of my life. And truth be told, I wanted him to die. The world, the faith, the church, and John's family would, in my opinion, be much improved if he just disappeared – but not like this.

"If I pull this trigger, I'll go to Hell," John said softly, "But it doesn't matter. I'm already there." Beads of sweat were rolling down his temple as they were mine. The Texas heat would make the Devil himself sweat.

"John, you do *not* want to do this. Think of your wife and kids–"

"But I'll go to Hell. Isn't suicide what a lot of people call the unforgivable sin?" he interrupted while ignoring my admonishment. What a selfish jerk. He cared more about himself than what a suicide would do to his wife and kids.

"Yeah, some say that's the unforgivable sin," I admitted. He continued to grip the Remington 12-gauge tightly. "But the unforgivable sin," I continued carefully, "is blasphemy against the Holy Spirit."

"So suicide *isn't* the unforgivable sin?" John continued to question.

"What? You want me to tell you that it is okay to kill yourself? Forget it, man. Taking your own life is a sin that you'll never be able to repent of. It's a sin unto death."

"I guess it would be," he admitted. I could smell the beer on his breath. He lit another cigarette contemplating his next move. His cigarette smoke repulsed me and he knew that, too. He just didn't care.

The depth of John's discouragement, depression, alcohol abuse, anger at God and the loss of his faith due to his desire to live a sinful lifestyle was literally overwhelming his mind and body. His spirit, at this point, was completely broken.

Even though John was a member of the Lord's church, he was now at a mental impasse and he believed that killing himself was the best option for his family.

Suicide, in my mind, was a cowardly way out, and a weakness that sickened me to the core.

"Michael, I have nothing left."

"What are you talking about? You've got everything! A beautiful wife that loves you and has forgiven you for everything! Terrific kids that think you're the greatest guy on the planet–"

"Don't be stupid, Michael. I've failed them in every way possible," he cut me off in a loud, angry growl.

"Shhh – lower your voice," I said.

"I'm sorry. Michael, when we got baptized, I never thought I'd turn out like this–"

"You can *change* your life, John!" I interrupted. Another verse flashed through my mind: *your sins will find you out.*

"Maybe," he said, "But I'm *beyond* forgiveness."

"That's ridiculous," I pushed forward, hoping to reach his heart in some way. "God can and *will* forgive you if you'll just trust in Him again. You know how the father responded in the story of the Prodigal Son. He said his son was lost but was found when the son came back home to him–"

"Hey! I've done a *lot* worse than the son in that story. God will never take me back," John said with a mixture of fear and disgust. "You *know* that, Michael!"

Complete despair. John had convinced himself that all hope for salvation was lost. My mind reeled and I thought of my friend Alan. He once said, "Christians who've fallen back into sin will sometimes limit the power of the blood. They tell themselves that Christ's blood will forgive everyone *else's* sins except their own."

"No, John, I *don't* know that! What I *do* know is that you still believe every word of the Bible. I know that you've gotten discouraged and bitter and angry with God, but that doesn't mean that He won't forgive you–"

"Listen, Michael. I've failed the Lord. I've brought reproach upon His name and His church. I've failed my family spiritually, financially, and emotionally. I've betrayed my marriage vows. I'm back to smoking, drinking, drugs, pornography – all of it! And God doesn't care…

I'm just another speck among six billion specks on this planet."

"John, He still loves you–"

"Yeah, everyone says that," John interrupted. "Michael, I just can't do it anymore," he said as he slowly turned his back toward the garage door. He raised the gun to his chin.

"No!" I screamed. At that moment the door from the garage to the laundry room opened…

Chapter 2
"We'll Save 'em All!"
April 1988 (16 years before): Nashville, Tennessee

Jonetta and I were new Christians, having been baptized into Christ just a few weeks before. We had started attending at a church of Christ in Bellevue, because it was only a quarter mile from our apartment complex.

The congregation had about nine hundred members, so we were pretty impressed that Carter Walker had even *found* us that first Sunday morning. Carter Walker was the Minister of Evangelism and Evan Thomas was the Pulpit Minister.

Carter introduced himself and discovered that we were new "babes in Christ."

"Michael and Jonetta, we have a series of full-color filmstrips that I would love to share with you. Each filmstrip comes with a workbook, and the series will take you all the way through the Bible; it begins with Genesis and ends with Revelation!

"These films – just five of them – will show you all of the main stories and divisions of the Bible. You'll find out where most of today's denominations came from, the plan of salvation, and the Lord's church – all in a visual format!

"And here's the best part. You'll get a certificate of completion when we're finished!"

You'd have to be a moron to turn this down, I thought to myself.

"Brother, we'd love to see 'em!" Uh-oh. Answering for Jonetta wasn't always the smartest thing to do. "Sorry, honey. *I'd* like to see them. What do you think?" I asked as I turned toward Jonetta.

"I'd love to see them, too!" Jonetta replied enthusiastically.

We were impressed with Carter's zeal and eagerness to teach us.

Five weeks later:

"Wow!" I leaned back on the couch in Carter Walker's office at the church building. "That's got to be one of the coolest things I've *ever* seen!" I said. Jonetta, sitting beside me, was smiling and shaking her head in the affirmative. We had just finished the last of the five Jule Miller filmstrips.

"I knew you'd like it," replied Carter.

"So, is this what *all* you church-uh-Christ people do?" I questioned with excitement while pointing to the old Bell and Howell film projector. Church-uh-Christ, said quickly as if it were one word, was simply the way I pronounced the name of the

Lord's church. Mature Christians said it correctly – church of
Christ.

"What do you mean?" Carter laughed as he responded.

"You know, showing these filmstrips to people?" I asked
very seriously, feeling as though I had missed the joke.

"Of course," Carter responded with humility and sincerity.
"Many in the church make the mistake of thinking that baptism
into Christ is like a finish line.

"In reality it is the beginning of the journey. You and
Jonetta are like new born babes in the Lord. Can you imagine any
loving parent putting their baby out in the world with no food,
water, or care?"

"That would be abandonment," Jonetta responded.

"That's right, Jonetta, and when we immerse souls into
Christ without feeding, nurturing, providing for them and taking
our time to help them grow and mature, it's a type of spiritual
abandonment.

"Christians never want to make the mistake of thinking
that baptism automatically makes a person knowledgeable and
faithful. Members of the church seem to think that when a person
is baptized they know it all, and they'll come to every service!

"*All* of us have a responsibility to teach every new soul in
Christ and help them to grow." Carter's points made perfect

sense. Church of Christ members were out showing these filmstrips, teaching the lost and making disciples.

"Alright," I said while standing up and pulling out my wallet. "Let me buy a projector and a set of filmstrips–"

"No, no, Michael! Put your money away!" Carter smiled and stood up with me. "If you're willing to show these to the lost, the church will take care of everything you need!" He seemed as excited as we were.

"Well whatchu waitin' on, man? Load us up!" I exclaimed. The three of us laughed loudly. He helped us carry the items out to our car. I popped the trunk and we loaded it up with a big stack of Jule Miller workbooks, a projector that felt like it weighed about forty pounds, and a brand new set of Jule Miller Filmstrips that had never even been opened.

"He must think you're pretty special," Jonetta whispered to me as we loaded the trunk.

"Why do you say that?" I whispered back.

"Because he's just given you a *brand-new* set of these films!" she replied.

"Hey, woman! My amazing third-grade education impressed him!" I whispered back.

She started laughing. "Oh yeah, you're an impressive…"

I waited. "An impressive what?" I asked.

"Moron!" She laughed and squealed! She loved to tease me.

"Hey, hey, little lady! Sticks and stones!" I shot back at her.

Nashville's WKRN News played in the background back at our tiny apartment. I was on the couch with my feet up on our glass-top coffee table writing the last two pages of my large, spiral-bound notebook.

"What are you doing?" Jonetta asked softly from the hallway.

"Finishing my journal notes of our conversion story. It contains pretty much everything that has happened to us over the past eight months. Want to know the title?"

"Yeah," Jonetta replied.

I held up the notebook's front cover so that she could see the title.

Conversion Story: 1988

"Wow! How original!" She said with a big laugh.

"Hey now! Don't make fun of my lack of imagination!" I said with as much seriousness as I could muster. "Didn't anyone ever tell you not to judge a book by its cover?"

She smiled and listened.

"You know what else I'm doing?" I continued.

"What?" she asked.

"Making a list of prospects to show these Jule Miller films to," I answered while searching for my ragged list of names. "Honey, do you know there's about five hundred thousand people in Nashville?" I said as I looked up at her standing in our small hallway.

"Sweetheart," she tried to get my attention.

"And do you realize that most of them *haven't* seen what we've seen–"

"Sweetheart," she tried again.

"Think of the possibilities–" I was rambling.

"Sweetheart," she said a third time, finally grabbing my attention.

"I'm sorry," finally looking up at her. "What?"

"Come to bed. It's late." She stood there in the hallway wearing a pair of Southern Illinois University sweatpants and an oversized Mickey Mouse T-shirt.

"Okay, just a few more minutes." I had some more names to add to the prospect list. Jonetta headed toward the bedroom as my mind continued to race…

Jesus had twelve disciples. If we showed these films to twelve people, and they showed twelve, and so on, and so on, all of Nashville will see the gospel in the next six months! Wow, that's a lot of projectors.

"Michael?" Jonetta was back in the living room. She had a second thought and had done a U-turn in the hallway. "I meant to tell you that the invitation to the Annual Spring Block Party came today, but I threw it away–"

"You what?" I interrupted. Our apartment complex threw a big party every spring in the grassy knoll right behind our building. About a hundred residents always attended. There would be BBQ, Coleslaw, a little Wang Chung and lots of beer.

"Michael, we're *not* going to that party now that we're–"

"Oh yes we are! We're going!" I interrupted her.

"No we're not! Christians aren't supposed to go to things like that–"

"Jonetta, listen. We'll go, eat BBQ, drink *iced-tea* and–"

"And what?" She interrupted as her anger grew.

"*And* we'll show 'em the Jule Miller filmstrips!"

"At a *beer* party? Michael, have you lost your mind?"

Thirty minutes later she was sound asleep. I, on the other hand, was swimming in my mind. *Five hundred thousand people... we'll save 'em all.* Those were my thoughts as I mulled over my growing list of names.

The materialistic dreams of seven figure incomes, a mansion in Brentwood, stock options, and BMW's were being replaced with very *different* dreams.

Dreams of saving souls.

Yes, it's true. Young, naïve, immature babes in Christ dream of saving the whole world. And would you like to know the real kicker in the story? I actually believed it was possible!

With men it is impossible, but with God all things are possible.

We were about to discover a shocking reality: not everyone shared our excitement about the gospel.

Chapter 3
Evangelism and... Beer?
August 1988

The previous four months of trying to evangelize had proven to be both exciting and bizarre.

We went to the Annual Spring Block Party. Jonetta and I mingled, drank iced tea, and waited. I couldn't start the filmstrips until dark. My nerves were on edge and my mouth was dry. Could I really do this? I *had* to find the courage because souls were at stake.

The crowd had grown throughout the evening to about a hundred. John Mellencamp was playing on a boom-box by the pool. Most of the food was gone, but the beer continued to flow and I fought the urge to drink. A cold beer sounded so good!

Temptation doesn't leave after you've been buried with Christ; actually, it probably gets a little worse. James said,

> *But every man is tempted, when he is drawn away of his own lust, and enticed. Then when lust hath conceived, it bringeth forth sin: and sin, when it is finished, bringeth forth death* (James 1:14-15).

So here we were at a big beer party, a party that would serve as the *initiation* of our evangelistic efforts. Jonetta talked with friends while I quickly carried equipment from the trunk of our car to the south end of the party area, far away from the swimming pool filled with intoxicated party goers and bikini-clad women.

The projector was set up on a TV tray with the cassette player at its side, both plugged into a long extension cord. I had sixty Lesson 1 workbooks in a Gestetner paper box and a new, six-foot tall by five-foot wide, portable screen.

"Can I have your attention?" I beckoned to the crowd while motioning for one of the drunks to turn down the music. He was kind enough to try to find the volume knob, but after a few moments with no success, he yanked the power cord out of the boom-box.

Jonetta began handing out the workbooks to the crowd while I spoke. The expressions on their faces were a mix of shock and confusion.

"Most of you know me–"

"What's goin' on, Shank?" One of the guys loudly interrupted somewhere from the crowd.

"I'm gonna show you something that's gonna change your life!" I responded with excitement and overwhelming fear.

"Do we gotta stop drinking?" A female voice questioned and the crowd roared with laughter.

"Uh," I stammered and the laughter increased. "Well, go ahead and drink. Just shut up and listen!"

To my surprise, the crowd grew deathly quiet. I switched on the projector and pushed the play button on the cassette player. The screen lit up and the voice of Texas Stevens thundered from the boom-box.

Wow! A hundred drunks watching Lesson #1 of Jule Miller's Visualized Bible Study Series!

The one-hour filmstrip came to the end. I stood up and turned around to face the crowd, expecting to announce the date, time, and location of filmstrip number two's presentation to a hundred people. The crowd had escaped! Six people remained. Workbooks were strewn across the complex's manicured lawn. I looked at Jonetta, feeling as though I was about to break down in tears. She mouthed the words, "It is okay. I love you."

In the excitement, along with my fear of messing up the timing between the audio narration from the cassette player and cranking the projector to each frame of the film, I hadn't paid attention to the mass exodus behind me.

The remaining six were kind-hearted neighbors who promised to come to the next filmstrip presentation.

None of them came back. And, needless to say, we didn't get invited to any more Annual Spring Block Parties.

We showed the Jule Miller filmstrips over the months that followed to anyone with a pulse and a body temperature: the Dominos Pizza guy, friends, co-workers, people we'd meet at gas stations – anybody who'd give us half a chance and a few minutes of their time.

I was busy trying to follow our Lord's command of going forth and preaching the gospel to every creature. There was no doubt in my mind that people thought I'd gotten myself into some kind of cult, but I didn't care. All of my brothers and sisters in Christ were out showing the gospel filmstrips, and Jonetta and I wanted to do our part.

Even though we worked hard at trying to win souls to Christ, we had little success, and our lack of success was my fault. I was new to the Lord's church and desperately needed spiritual growth. In addition, my approach was horrible. I pushed the gospel onto people who had no real interest in the message.

Fortunately, we were growing spiritually. Jonetta and I loved attending the Bible classes and worship services at Bellevue. Several young couples in the congregation befriended us and made it a point to include us in many spiritual activities, which helped us become more grounded in our new faith.

But I was about to discover a disturbing secret. It was a secret that would kill my zeal and derail my desire to share the gospel with anyone...

Chapter 4
Burned Bulbs

September 1988

"Brother Carter!" I greeted him as we met one another at the building.

"Hello, Brother Mike!" Carter was always upbeat and smiling. His deft hands worked the lock to the door of the church building, and seconds later we walked briskly through the church building toward his office. The place always smelled good.

"I really appreciate you meeting me up here this evening. Carter, this is the fifth light bulb I've blown up in as many months." I explained, with curiosity as to why they didn't last very long.

"Don't worry about it, Mike," Carter replied. "These projector bulbs are made to burn very bright, but they also put off a lot of heat. I think that's why they don't last long."

We reached his office and he retrieved a new projector bulb from a tall, double-door cabinet. As he handed me the bulb, I noticed that the price tag had been left on the box. $21.95.

"Whoa, wait a minute, Carter," I said while holding out my right hand in a *stop* gesture.

"What's the matter, Mike?"

"Carter, this bulb costs the church twenty-two bucks?"

"Yeah, but it is okay, Mike. We've got to have them," Carter replied.

"But hang on, Carter." I couldn't get my mind around the apparent problem. "I'm not stupid. If everyone is blowing one of these bulbs every month like I am, there's no way the church can afford to keep doing this!"

"Uh… how many people do you think are out showing the Jule Miller films, Mike?" Carter asked with sincere concern.

"Well, let's see… there are about four hundred men in this congregation, so I'd say four hundred. Carter, that's four hundred bulbs every month multiplied by twenty two bucks a bulb – the bulbs alone are costing the church about eighty-eight hundred a month, right?" I asked, having no doubt about my mathematical abilities.

"Michael, we don't have four hundred men showing the filmstrips." Carter looked ashamed. "We don't have anywhere *close* to that number."

"How many people are showing them, Carter?"

He held up two fingers.

It was like getting hit in the stomach by a line drive.

"What? You are kidding me," I responded in shock.

"Michael, I wish I were," said Carter with visible sadness.

"Well, it's me, and who else?" I asked.

"Me," Carter admitted. "Mike, it's you and me."

It only took a couple of minutes to drive back to our apartment. I went straight to the kitchen calendar without saying a word to Jonetta.

"What's wrong?" Jonetta asked with visible concern.

"Hang on just a sec," I said. The terse response made her more concerned. The date on our calendar, which was held to our refrigerator with a plethora of magnets, was Thursday, September 8, 1988. Our appointment to show a nice young couple the filmstrips was written on the calendar, scheduled for 7:00pm. I looked at my watch. 6:38pm.

"Honey, tell me what's going on," Jonetta pressed me.

"I will, but I've got to call this couple real quick." I dialed their number, and they picked up.

"Hi, this is Michael Shank. We've got a Bible study appointment at seven, but I can't make it tonight. I'm really sorry, but something has come up."

The man was gracious regarding the cancellation, especially on such short notice. I told them we would reschedule and we ended the call. It was a lie. I would never reschedule the appointment.

"Now tell me what's happened!" Jonetta was worried and getting more impatient by the minute.

We sat down. I told her that Carter and I were the *only* two people in the entire congregation showing the Jule Miller films.

"You are the only two?"

"Yeah."

"The only two in the whole church?"

"Yeah."

"But why'd you cancel tonight's Bible study?" She asked.

"Evidently those brethren at Bellevue know *something* that we don't, and I'm not showing any more films until we find out what that *something* is."

Chapter 5
We Have Nothing to Fear But...
September 1988

"Michael, it is fear," Carter said to me as we sat on the old couch his office at the Bellevue church building. I had arrived here unannounced, coming directly from my office after work – on the hunt for that *something* that caused only two out of nine hundred Christians in a congregation to actively share the gospel. "Fear keeps people from sharing the gospel."

"Fear of what?" I asked.

"Fear of questions," he answered. "Fear of questions and a lack of knowledge. Brother, we have gotten away from really studying and memorizing God's Word. When people fail to build a strong knowledge of the Bible, they *fear* bringing it up to others."

"Then why don't they study?" I asked. Things seem pretty black and white when you're young and naïve.

Carter smiled, "That's the question, Michael," he said as he jumped up from the couch. "Let's go get something to eat!"

He'd heard my stomach growling.

"Let's do it!" I said without hesitation.

Bellevue's Pizza Inn was packed. It was always jammed up on Friday nights. I'd made three trips to the buffet and had finally finished a slice of dessert pizza – ham and pineapple. The waitress had just topped offed our drinks.

"Carter, what do we do?" I was discouraged.

"Michael, it's been a fundamental challenge for the last few decades. Life is busier now. People are caught in their daily grind: careers, kids, ballgames, ballet practice, television–"

"Those are just excuses," I interrupted.

"Yeah, you're right. But that's the reality of the life we live today. I'm not defending the excuses, Michael. I'm only pointing out the obstacles that we have to deal with. Your willingness to go out and share the gospel has been a boon to the brethren–"

"I was only doing what *you* said *everyone else* was doing," interrupting a second time.

"I said *everyone* was showing the Jule Miller filmstrips?" he asked with complete confusion.

"Yeah. After that last filmstrip, I asked you if this is what all you church-uh-Christ people did, and you said it was," I said defensively.

"Ah, Michael. I'm sorry. I thought you were asking if showing the filmstrips was something *you* should be doing. I didn't realize I gave you the impression that *everyone* in the church was doing filmstrip Bible studies."

"It's okay, Carter. I'm sorry I misunderstood."

"Michael," said Carter, "don't get discouraged. Your excitement about sharing the gospel is contagious. I don't think you realize the positive effect you're having on the brethren at Bellevue–"

"So what!" I interrupted a third time. "It's not causing them to *do* anything, is it?"

"Michael, don't let anyone's inactivity dictate your passion for the lost." He pulled out his Bible. "Let me show you Mark 4." He found the reference and began to read,

> *And he said unto them, Know ye not this parable? and how then will ye know all parables? The sower soweth the word. And these are they by the way side, where the word is sown; but when they have heard, Satan cometh immediately, and taketh away the word that was sown in their hearts. And these are they likewise which are sown on stony ground; who, when they have heard the word, immediately receive it with gladness; And have no root in themselves, and so endure but for a time: afterward, when affliction or persecution ariseth for the word's sake, immediately they are offended. And these are they which are sown among thorns; such as hear the word, and the cares of this world, and the deceitfulness of riches, and the lusts of other things*

entering in, choke the word, and it becometh

unfruitful. And these are they which are sown on

good ground; such as hear the word, and receive it,

and bring forth fruit, some thirtyfold, some sixty,

and some an hundred (Mark 4:13-20).

"Michael, the church's biggest challenge is described here in verse 19,

And the cares of this world, and the deceitfulness of

riches, and the lusts of other things entering in,

choke the word, and it becometh unfruitful.

"The cares of this present world choke out the study of God's Word. Ignorance of the Word causes fear to discuss the Word with the lost."

"Cares of this present world choke out the Word," I repeated while staring at the pizza buffet. "Carter, how do we get our brothers and sisters to study?"

"Encouragement, little brother. We become like Barnabas."

"Who's Barnabas?" I asked.

"Well," Carter explained, "he's in Acts 4. His name was Joseph but they started calling him Barnabas, because Barnabas meant *son of encouragement*." Carter stood up, threw a five dollar bill on the table for the tip, put his arm around me, and said, "Now come on, Barnabas. We've got a lot of work to do."

As we walked by the buffet I grabbed one last slice of ham and pineapple. He gave me a funny look.

"Hey," I laughed, "It's for the road!"

"You might want to study gluttony!" Said Carter as he laughed his way out of the restaurant door.

"Yeah, well, you're no Barnabas, yourself!" I responded.

However, storm clouds were brewing... *spiritual* storm clouds.

Chapter 6
Ever Had a Finger Up Your Nose?
March 1991

The last three years had been the happiest of our lives. The Bellevue congregation had proven to be a great blessing toward grounding us in the faith and helping us to grow spiritually. While we were admittedly still growing (and needed a lot more growth), we had each made tremendous strides.

Jonetta loved the variety of Bible studies offered at Bellevue, and she had made several close friendships. We participated in almost every function the church offered: services three times each week, area-wide singings, a young married couples group, a weekly home Bible study group-potluck, and our weekly evening to show new prospects the Jule Miller filmstrips.

I had overcome cigarettes, alcohol, cursing, and lust of the flesh. Well, at least I tried my best to turn away from gawking at the bodies of scantily clad girls during the summertime. And no, I wasn't always successful, but I tried my best.

We were certainly *not* perfect, but we had both grown beyond what we'd thought would ever be possible.

Our marriage was, to put it simply, happier. We were husband and wife, but also a spiritual brother and sister to one another. We discussed our spiritual problems, victories, doubts, and hopes. Jonetta and I read the Bible together, prayed together, and encouraged one another. My materialistic, worldly nature had dissolved.

A deep sense of peace through Jesus Christ enveloped us and was fostered by all of these spiritual and physical things we did together. It was that peace that Paul spoke of,

> *Rejoice in the Lord alway: and again I say,*
> *Rejoice. Let your moderation be known unto all*
> *men. The Lord is at hand. Be careful for nothing;*
> *but in everything by prayer and supplication with*
> *thanksgiving let your requests be made known*
> *unto God. And the peace of God, which passeth all*
> *understanding, shall keep your hearts and minds*
> *through Christ Jesus* (Philippians 4:4-7).

And there was another thing… John. John, my best friend since the age of thirteen, hadn't been around for several years after our baptism. Yes, there were times I missed him, but I was glad we were no longer as close.

"That's it!" Jonetta said. We had just loaded the last box into the U-Haul. I kissed Andrew, our first child, on the forehead. Why do babies always smell so good?

Jonetta was holding him in her arms. He was wearing a sock hat and a tiny blue Land's End jacket… what a beautiful kid! He looked just like her – big blue eyes and long eyelashes.

As we stood there in our small apartment, tears began to roll down our cheeks. Our apartment was empty, clean and ready to be rented to someone else. I had my final paycheck in one pocket, and our refunded security deposit in the other.

We were moving back to southern Illinois. It was bittersweet. We had decided, after the birth of Andrew, that it would be better to raise our children in a smaller community close to family.

Our parents would enjoy the opportunity to be involved grandparents. We would have the support structure of extended family. And Jonetta and I could help the small, flailing church of Christ back home. It seemed to make sense for all of the right reasons.

"Jonetta, is this the right thing to do?"

"Michael, only God knows the answer to that question." She hugged me tightly. Andrew, being squished between us, took the opportunity to poke his little finger up my nose.

"Drew!" I hollered and grabbed his hand. Jonetta laughed so hard she almost dropped him. He started to cry, and I took him from her arms apologizing to him while kissing his cheeks.

"Jonetta," I said between kissing his face, "please get that booger off his finger before I get sick!"

We pulled out of the apartment complex, took a left onto Highway 70 South, and then drove up onto I-40 East. Twenty-six minutes later we were on I-24 west… headed to Eldorado, Illinois with different dreams this time.

What do they say about hind sight?

Chapter 7
"I'm Back!"
July 1992

It was now July, 1992.

"Brother Mike, good to see you this evening," Charles said with a formal smile and a firm hand-shake. It was his standard greeting for everyone. We had been back in southern Illinois for 17 months, and we had just had our second child, Paul.

"Good to see you again, Brother Charles," I replied in kind. The humidity in southern Illinois was horrible. We had only walked 40 feet from the car to the front door of the little, white-washed, cinder-block church building, and the perspiration covered us.

"Hot, Daddy!" Andrew said.

"Yes it is, honey," I answered him.

I had Andrew in my arms, while Jonetta held Paul. We stepped into the foyer of the little building and greeted the brethren – all nine of them. Yes – nine.

We'd been living in a rental house in Eldorado for the past 17 months, but the closing was almost complete on our first home. It was a modest home in the country a few miles south of Harrisburg, close to Jonetta's parents' home.

I was working as a computer consultant 29 minutes north of Eldorado. Microsoft Windows 3.1 had just been released a few months before, and business was busy. It was a prestigious job, but that's as far as it went. I had a suit and tie, a briefcase, and an important-sounding title, but it was a job that didn't pay well and had almost no benefits. However, it was still a good job for southern Illinois. We looked good and smelled good, but we were broke.

Jonetta was a full-time mother, and we did everything that we could do to survive. The mortgage on the house was going to be a little cheaper than the rent we were paying, so that would help a little.

Evening service began with singing. Four men, seven women, a two year old boy, and a four month old boy. We were the only family under sixty-five years of age.

Ed led the singing. Charles had just stepped into the pulpit to deliver the evening sermon, and I would serve at the Lord's Table after the sermon. Phil would be called on to lead the closing prayer.

Two minutes into the sermon I was looking at my watch. I was ashamed of my behavior, but Charles' sermons were typed out manuscripts, and he read them word-for-word without looking up.

"Hey, Jonetta," I whispered. "Can we leave quickly tonight?"

"Uh, sure. Why?" she asked.

"I'm just not in the mood for any *after* service visiting."

"Okay," she said with concern but without surprise. "Are you okay, Michael?"

"Oh, yeah. I'm fine. Just a little tired. I'm going to go get a drink of water. Can I sit Andrew here against you?"

"Sure, honey. Sit him here."

I got up, went to the foyer, and sipped from the water fountain. It was so cold it'd freeze your teeth. I stood up, wiped the corner of my mouth, turned around, and froze… John was standing there! I hadn't even heard the door–

"Why are *you* here? *Here* of all places?"

"Relax, Michael. How long has it been?"

"About four years," I said in the most melancholy way.

"Look, I've been wanting to see you–"

"John, I don't want to hear it–" I interrupted.

"Michael, you know I've been in town for a few weeks–"

"Yeah, and you show up *here*? At *worship*?" My frustration was growing by the second.

"Listen, I figured you needed a friend, and you know we go back a long way," he responded.

I'd met John at the age of thirteen. It was in the eighth grade, and I was in Social Studies staring at the legs of a girl wearing shorts that were beyond short. That's when John leaned over and whispered something about her legs. At that moment we became friends.

"Not now, John. Just leave." I turned around toward the entrance to the auditorium. Everyone seemed fixated on Charles' sermon.

"Michael," he whispered. "Meet me tomorrow night."

"Where?" I asked quickly in an effort to get rid of him. John told me and left.

He's back. Dear God, what now?

Charles wrapped up his sermon in his usual way - a very unexcited, monotone rendition of the plan of salvation. Then we sang the same invitation song that we sang every week, *Just as I Am*.

I served the Lord's Table, but there was no one there who hadn't taken communion that morning. Phil led the closing prayer by praying for growth and to keep us until the next appointed hour. I felt like I was going to vomit.

"Michael, you're pale. Are you sure you're alright?" Jonetta asked as she looked at my face.

"Yeah, yeah, I'm fine. Let's just go." She was holding Paul and stepped out into the aisle. I picked up Andrew, grabbed the diaper bag, and we hot-footed it out of the building.

We walked past the yard sign toward our car. The sign said, "A church of Christ Meets Here."

The feeling overwhelmed me.

It was a feeling of fear.

Chapter 8
"Show Me the Money!"

The Next Night

John and I had been baptized during the same time, but I hadn't seen him since. He and Rose had also moved back to southern Illinois.

"Well if you're as broke as I am, you'd better do it," John encouraged. It was about 11:00pm, and the bright lights from the McDonald's parking lot shined down onto the dashboard of my minivan.

"I've got to do *something*!" I said in despair.

"Yes, you do, and so do I," John replied. "We'll do it together! You sponsor me, okay?"

"I'll call him tonight," I said as I started the engine.

"Hey, back in business! Partners again!" John was ecstatic. I pulled out onto Highway 45 ignoring John and his new-found enthusiasm. The house was about ten minutes south. I would drop him off in a few minutes then I could *really* think about this so-called business opportunity.

Moving back to southern Illinois was proving to be a poor decision. Jonetta and I were about to slip into bankruptcy. A Chapter 7 bankruptcy would allow us the option to reaffirm on the house and car, thus keeping both, but we still wouldn't be making enough money to pay everyone back.

My prestigious computer job didn't pay enough to cover our living expenses *and* cover our existing monthly debts. Additionally, the minivan's tires were bald and the engine was six-thousand miles overdue for the routine oil change.

To make matters worse, we had been forced to sign up for food stamps the previous week. Food stamps... us? What in the world had happened? I was on my way to great success in Nashville – a big BMW, several homes, trips, boats, a large salary with stock options – wasn't that the dream? Now, here we were on food stamps.

I gritted my teeth and cursed under my breath. John laughed loudly. Few things in life damage a man's self-worth more than having to put his family on food stamps.

As we struggled to cover the most basic of life's needs, we were exhausted emotionally and starving spiritually. The brethren at the little church of Christ were good people who were trying their best, but the robotic routine, their constant negative talk about why we were not growing, and a lack of fellowship outside of the regular services had taken a deep toll on us.

Discouragement had led me to stop doing the two most important things in the life of a Christian – prayer and study.

Why would any Christian stop praying? Because discouraged Christians fall into resentment. Resentment leads to doubt. Doubt leads to disbelief. Disbelief leads one to stop praying. Why would you pray when disbelief dominates your heart (disbelief of the power of God, His Word, prayer, etc.)? Furthermore, why would someone spend time talking to one they resent?

And study? Men and women rarely invest their time in things they feel will not benefit them. In other words, people do things when there is a payoff. People do *not* tend to do things if there is no payoff. At least that's what Zig Ziglar said.

And when you begin to resent God and start to believe that God's Word has no benefit, it becomes almost impossible to read it.

"Michael," John wanted my attention.

"What?"

"God has favorites," he said, "and *we* ain't them."

"How about you shut up until we get there?" I was agitated. We were only about a minute from his house, and I couldn't wait to get rid of him for the evening.

"All I'm doing is verbalizing an observational effect of a truth that can be visualized and proven in every culture and every region of the world. That observational affect is this – God plays favorites."

I listened.

"Consider those around you Michael. They have no affinity for the One God of Heaven; yet, they're blessed in their careers, their social life, and their status in the community. And *we* can't even pay our bills."

"John, the Bible says that God's blessings rain on the just and the unjust. My decisions are not His fault, and the fact that I've made my own free-will decisions doesn't implicate God's responsibility!"

"Michael, I'm just saying that you have been faithful. Where has it got you? Broke? Unhappy?"

"John, we're here. Get out."

I pulled into my driveway and went inside. Jonetta was fast asleep. Andrew was in his bed with his little arms wrapped around a Winnie-the-Pooh that was bigger than he was. Paul's crib was next to Andrew's bed. He stirred a bit when I kissed his head, but he didn't wake up. I squeezed his diaper; it didn't feel like he had peed in it.

I put a couple of oak splits into the wood-burner. The living room felt like toast. Our little home was modest, but Jonetta kept it clean and comfortable.

The "business opportunity" dominated my thoughts. Thank God John was gone, and I had time to think. Eddie said that I could get in for $100.00. That would pay for my starter kit, and then I could begin to sponsor people.

"Build an organization," he said. "That's where the big money is!" The company was a very well-known multi-level marketing company that sold soap. I'd never heard of it, but it seemed legit. They had evolved into some type of wholesale-resale company, but the way you made big money was to sponsor other people and build an organization *under* you. Those you sponsored would, in turn, sponsor people under them.

It was a pyramid that, theoretically, grew under you so that you would generate a small profit from every person in your organization. Eddie had explained that we could work five to ten hours each week and make six-figures a year in the next two to five years, depending on how hard we worked. He called it the "2-5 year plan."

I was young, impressionable, and hungry for financial success. It was 11:43pm. Time to call Eddie.

"Eddie, it's Mike," I said into the phone.

"Hey, Mike! Great to hear from you! Man, I was just talking about you!"

"Oh yeah?" I asked. His enthusiasm was contagious.

"Absolutely, man! You are one of the sharpest guys I've ever met, and I know you'd be great in this business!"

"Well, uh, thanks a lot, Eddie. That's why I wanted to call and I'm really sorry it's so late–"

"It's never too late to talk to a real winner like you, Mike!" Eddie replied. His gift of gab was incredible. Was I *this* special, or did he say this to everyone he was trying to sponsor?

"Thanks, Eddie. Hey, I'm in!" I replied, trying desperately to meet his level of enthusiasm.

"Man, you're awesome! You are a winner, and I knew you wouldn't pass up on the best business this world has ever seen! You'll be a direct distributor in no time, brother!"

If God wouldn't help me, I would have to find a way to do it on my own.

Chapter 9
Wanna Dance?
October 1994

October: 1994.

It had been a little over two years since John and I had held our McDonald's parking lot meeting. We had spent the past two years working like brainwashed animals to "build the business," following every instruction of our up-line's 2-5 year plan.

John and Rose had just pulled into their driveway late in the evening after visiting a mall in Paducah, Kentucky.

"No, God, no!"

The fireman who had tackled John pressed him against the cold, wet grass and mud of his front yard. John had jumped out of his car and sprinted toward the front door of his burning home.

"Just let me get the pictures—"

"John, it's too late! It's too late, man – you can't go in," replied the fireman trying to hold John down. "It's all gone!"

Rose dropped to the ground. Her two boys wept in her arms at the edge of the driveway. They watched through tears as the flames burst through the roof at the north end of the home. The smoke was strange, not like trash burning, but something else.

"John," a local fireman, someone John knew from High School, asked, "Where can y'all go tonight?"

He rubbed the tears from his eyes and looked at Rose.

"My mom and dad's," Rose replied.

"That's good. Do NOT try to go back in. Do you understand me, John?" the fireman stated. "John, do you hear me?"

"Yeah." John replied.

"John, do I have your word?"

"Yeah, you've got my word." John said.

The house was a total loss. Burned beyond recognition. Fire investigators found that their old electric stove's rear-right knob hadn't been turned completely to the off position when John and Rose left the house to go to the mall. That rear-right burner held an iron skillet with a small amount of bacon grease – just enough to start the fire that destroyed their home.

"Michael, I need to talk," John begged.

"Where?" I asked.

"Centerfield. Eight pm." John said.

Cigarette smoke hung in the air as Led Zeppelin played from the jukebox. Pool balls crashed in the background. Centerfield was the most popular bar in town.

"I'm glad we're here," John said as he lit a cigarette.

I sat and listened. Jonetta and I were clinging desperately to our faith, and I was uncomfortable in this environment. But John's

life was out of control, and I had no choice but to try to turn him
around.

"John, *please* don't smoke," I pleaded.

"Michael, smoking is the least of my worries. Do you
realize what I've done? What I've been through?"

"Yeah, I do, John," I said with confidence.

"Okay, boss! Tell me!" John was belligerent.

"No, John. I'll listen. You tell *me*."

A waitress brought John another beer. He was on his way
to a drunken stupor.

"You know as well as I do, Michael. Rose and I are broke,
and I've practically worked myself to death. We filed bankruptcy,
just lost our home and everything we had to a fire, and worst of
all…"

"Go ahead," I encouraged.

"I've committed adultery." Tears flowed from our eyes.

"John, we're Christian men," I said while looking down at
the cheap laminate on the bar.

"Michael, God does not love me. He doesn't want someone
like me. I've left Him and to be honest, I don't think He'll ever
forgive me for what I've done."

"John, God is a God of second chances."

"Hey, John! Wanna dance?" A woman hollered at him from the dance floor.

"Not with a skank!" John shouted without looking her direction. She flipped him the bird and danced a 180.

"Does Rose know?" I asked with surprise.

"Yes, and she's forgiven me. Can you believe that? She is *that* forgiving?"

"She's a woman beyond you, man!" I laughed.

"Yes, she is."

"Why are we here, John?" I asked sincerely.

"Michael, after two years of working the business with you [the pyramid business that Eddie introduced us to], I'm now a silver direct distributor, and it's a scam! We've worked the business 30 hours every week for the past two years – do you know how many people we have under us now?"

"Yeah, John. One hundred and thirty nine distributorships."

"Yeah, and do you know what I found out today?"

I listened.

"I found out that the real money is in selling all of the motivational books and tapes! Not the products! So do you know what I told Eddie?"

I just continued to listen.

"I told him that I quit! It's a scam, and I quit!"

"John, calm down." I encouraged.

"Michael, I've neglected my family for the past two years. Worked thirty hours a week outside of my regular job to build this stupid scam of a business and I didn't know it was a scam until today!

"Rose is so distant that we don't even know each other anymore. My boys don't know me. We've lost everything we have. Now I'm smoking and drinking, again."

"John, I know what's happened to you, but where are you going with this–"

"I'm telling you that God doesn't care about me or my family–"

"John, He does–"

"God does *NOT* care!" John interrupted and raised his voice. "And I need another beer!"

Chapter 10
Michael's Past Decade
February 2004

February, 2004:

A decade had passed for Jonetta and me. What happened to us over those past ten years?

We struggled to maintain what little faith we had left. When John came back into the picture, he and I decided to put our time and energy into trying to save our family from financial ruin.

We started a series of businesses that we partnered together. My energies went into making sure the businesses were successful, and working both day and night had taken a toll on my wife, family, friends, and my faith.

I had succumbed to discouragement, but it went much deeper than that. Jonetta and I had been mere "babes in Christ" when we moved back to southern Illinois. And, though we did not know at the time, we were not spiritually mature enough to survive leaving the strength and encouragement we received at the Bellevue congregation.

Leaving Bellevue had been impulsive, financially devastating, and spiritually toxic. What did James say about moving and uprooting?

> *Go to now, ye that say, To day or tomorrow we will go into such a city, and continue there a year, and buy and sell, and get gain: Whereas ye know not what shall be on the morrow. For what is your life?*

*It is even a vapor, that appeareth for a little time,
and then vanisheth away. **For that ye ought to say,
If the Lord will**, we shall live, and do this, or that*
(James 4:13-15).

After John appeared at the church building that evening in
July of `94, Jonetta and I, shortly thereafter, left that little church of
Christ congregation. During the following ten years, I would try to
encourage John, but I was spiritually weak… too weak do deal with
him.

My family and I visited many other local congregations, off
and on, without ever finding a real "fit."

It wasn't the church's fault. Most every congregation we
visited tried to make us feel welcomed, loved, and "at home."

It wasn't God's fault, for God was not a God of "shifting
loyalties" (James 1:17). Regardless of John's opinion that God had
"favorites," the Bible says otherwise. Acts 10:34-35 says,

*Then Peter opened his mouth, and said, Of a truth I
perceive that God is no respecter of persons: But in
every nation **he that feareth him, and worketh
righteousness, is accepted with him**.*

In reality, God never leaves or forsakes His children (Deut.
31:6). He loves us so much that He, while we were still sinners,
sent His son to die for us (Romans 5:8); and not our love for Him,

but His love for *us* caused Him to send His only Son to die for us (1 John 4:10).

We had removed ourselves from God's wonderful grace – that grace that every human craves, even when they can't quite put their finger on that "thing" they crave. We had removed ourselves from His grace by abandoning our first love: His Word.

Where does a man or woman find grace? When did it first appear? Titus 2:11-12 answers the question,

> *For the **grace of God that bringeth salvation hath appeared to all men, <u>teaching</u> us** that, denying ungodliness and worldly lusts, we should live soberly, righteously, and godly, in this present world.*

God's love and grace is something that is "taught" to us. And by what source are we taught God's grace? *For the law was given by Moses, **but grace and truth came by Jesus Christ*** (John 1:17). God's grace came through Jesus Christ, who was the Word and *is* the Word.

> *In the beginning was the Word, and the Word was with God, and the Word was God. The same was in the beginning with God. All things were made by him; and without him was not any thing made that*

was made.   In him was life; and the life was the
light of men (John 1:1-4).

The grace and love of God comes expressly through His
Son, Jesus Christ – the Word of God.   Acts 20:32 verifies this idea,
And now, brethren, I commend you to God, **and to**
the word of his grace, which is able to build you
up, and to give you an inheritance among all them
which are sanctified.

What had the past ten years done to John?

Chapter 11
John's Past Decade
February 2004: Same Time Frame

February 2004:

A decade had passed for John and Rose.

The past ten years had been different for John. He had grown into a man unrecognizable by friends and family. His physical appearance and attitude had completely morphed.

John had always been slight in stature. At the age of 18 he was 5'10" tall, weighed 125lbs and had a 30" waist. His size had always made him insecure about himself.

In 1995 an amateur bodybuilder introduced him to injectable anabolic steroids. One look at his friend's incredible physique instantly removed any personal fear connected to steroids.

After John's first cycle of steroids, he gained 30 pounds of muscle. At the end of his second cycle of steroids, he was much bigger. He weighed 193 lbs. and had a 31" waist. His chest was 45" and he was nothing but muscle.

He bleached his teeth and tanned regularly. John's objective was *look the best to be the best*. He wore the finest clothes, flashed the finest jewelry, and drove the best cars that money could buy.

While John "looked" great on the outside, his alcohol use led to experimentation with marijuana and cocaine. He had, at this point, been involved in nine bar-fights, resulting in him being beaten and bloodied in the majority of altercations, but never arrested.

Regardless of his extracurricular activities, the past ten years of partnering with Michael had been good for John. Their combined ability to start a business and to resell that business had proven to be financially successful.

John had also, by this point earned his education in Audiology. He had passed the Illinois State Board of Exams and obtained an Illinois license to practice audiology, and the clinical practice of dispensing hearing aids.

John had been operating a hearing practice in southern Illinois and was considered, by his boss, to be the most successful man in the company – at least that's what his boss told him. He had set the record for the most hearing aid sales in a year – in the history of the company.

But it wasn't enough for John. John hired eight telemarketers to set audiology appointments for the entire firm. He recruited and trained six highly-qualified people to become audiological hearing instrument specialists, all of whom had passed their board exams and were on their way to opening their own offices – offices that would line John's pockets with cash.

John was finally at the top of his game. He won awards for his performance. The company presented him with bonuses and all-expense-paid cruises for his accomplishments. But John was lost. He had left the Lord, the Lord's church, and his faith.

Michael would try his best to discuss the things of faith and to be an encouragement, but John wouldn't listen. John had become a powerhouse for Satan and materialism. He'd outgrown Michael in the worst way, and Michael had grown spiritually weak.

But John still knew the Word of God. John had studied the Word enough from his first few years after his baptism to know that he was lost. However, he clung to his spiritual discouragement as an excuse for his worldly lifestyle and sinful behavior.

John's pride, arrogance, and lifestyle were about to be brought to an end. *Pride goeth before destruction, and an haughty spirit before a fall* (Proverbs 16:18).

He had, through discouragement and resentment, turned his back on God. John had grown into a man who loved the pleasures of sin and he had brought reproach upon the name of Jesus Christ. So wouldn't the world be better off without him? Why wouldn't God simply snuff-out the life of someone as narcissistic, selfish, and evil as John?

As impossible as it may sound, God had a plan for the worthless human being known as John.

Chapter 12
Alone at Applebee's

April 2004

The Audiology firm John and Mike worked for had fallen into serious legal problems, and they could see the writing on the wall. The company was imploding, so they began the hunt to replace their high-income jobs.

Mike had received a call from a former contact and it seemed like an answer to their prayers. He would move to Dallas, Texas, establish a sales office in the health equipment industry with the parent company, and be back to a six-figure income within the year! The balance sheets, market data, and projection tables revealed the potential for a seven-figure annual income.

John and Mike moved to Texas to get their office and home established, planning to move their family to the area after everything was in place.

Each found a beautiful, upscale home in the same Lake Dallas subdivision. They signed a lease for a large office in Plano, and began the task of interviewing potential employees.

The two were quickened together by their spiritual discouragement and their mutual need to be financially successful. The need that drives all men is to provide for their families.

The Applebee's restaurant was about to bust at the seams with people. I half-expected an ambitious fire marshal to arrive at any moment and demand that half the crowd leave due to fire codes. I loved the baby-back ribs, and John loved the beer, so it was an easy decision. And truth be told, I needed to be around people. Missing Jonetta was horrible, but the chatter of the crowd helped to drown out my thoughts of her and the kids. We'd been there over an hour, and our food hadn't arrived.

"Michael, do you remember that big cop that stopped you and Jonetta that night y'all were going to be baptized?" John asked with a laugh. He wanted to reminisce.

"John," I sat my beer on the table, "that's one of the greatest memories of my life. I think of it often."

"I wonder what happened to your friend Larry. And Ryan? That was the guy you played racquetball with in Nashville," John said as he dug up good memories.

"Yeah," I laughed. "Larry? Wow, I haven't thought about Larry in a long time. Randall taught him the gospel first–"

"Yeah, I know–" John cut me off.

"Last I heard Larry was in South Carolina working in Information Technology. But Ryan…" John could see that my expression had turned sour.

"Ryan was killed in a car wreck a few years ago," I said with remorse.

"No way! Wait a minute… I remember that now."

"I was never able to persuade him to obey the gospel. His entire family were Episcopalians. You know, they went to that large Episcopalian Church in Belle Meade–"

"Yeah, yeah. I know," John said flatly. "What about Randall?"

"What about him?" I asked.

"Heard from him lately?" John knew the answer.

"John, don't be an idiot. I'd never want Randall to find out who I've become. "

"Hey, hey, Michael – you mean who *we've* become, don't you?"

"Oh, sorry to have hurt your feelings," I laughed. "Of course. Who *we've* become." The laugh was a ruse. The guilt and shame of my unfaithfulness to Christ was too much to bear.

John raised his bottle for a toast. "To great success in the Big D!"

We raised a bottle to the toast. No one seemed to notice. I sat back in my chair to finish an article in the latest edition of Diagnostic Imagining magazine while John ate cheese-sticks.

"You know, Michael, these little Mexican waitresses are sexy–"

"Shut up, John. All I want to think about is Jonetta and I don't want to hear any more of your sexual comments."

"Okay, okay. Just saying."

Back in southern Illinois, Rose was praying. John and Rose had experienced almost everything a married couple could endure. There were extreme ups and downs: a bankruptcy, extramarital affairs, job losses, the loss of their home to a fire, a car repossessed, great business success, big yearly incomes, the loss of those incomes, the loss of their faith in Jesus Christ, and their loss of Christian friends to support and encourage them. The stresses on their marriage seemed to oscillate with the peripheral extremes of their lives.

The opportunity in Dallas seemed like it might be the answer that Rose had been praying for. Even though "faith" had not been a part of their lives for many years, Rose still prayed. She still read the Bible, and she trusted John's business sense. Success would *surely* be found in Dallas, Texas!

Chapter 13
The Laundry Door Opened…
August, 2004: Lake Dallas, Texas

Five months after moving to Dallas.

Dallas had *not* been the answer, but more of a curse. The business was, at first, promising, but quickly proved to be an empty shell. John had moved Rose and their family into a 4,800 square-foot, brick home in a manicured Lake Dallas subdivision off of I-35 North at the Swisher Exit.

While John and Rose did everything in their power to maintain a successful suburban lifestyle, John was faltering. His business was operating in the red, he had laid off half of his staff, and their $1,700 a month lease payment on their home was no longer in their reach.

It was late in the evening. John stood in the large, dark living room in his underwear and an old T-shirt, trying to peak out of the large plantation windows facing the front lawn. All he could do was watch as the two men worked quickly in his driveway. Their heads darted around looking back and forth to see if anyone was coming. They had just completed winching John's Toyota Camry onto the slope of the flatbed wrecker. It was being repossessed. *Another* car repossessed. It would be the last time it happened.

Life was spinning out of control. The house was quiet. Rose and the children slept.

Michael was suffering from the same issues with their failing business. John decided to go see Michael… one last time.

John and Michael stood in Michael's garage. Sweat poured down Mike's face as he watched the gun in John's hands. Mike had been trying to calm John down – trying in some way to get him to see that he had other options.

John said, "I just can't do it anymore."

He raised the gun to his chin–

"No!" Mike screamed in his mind. At that moment the door from the garage to the laundry room opened…

Chapter 14
Dr. Jekyll &
Mr. Hyde
Same Place – Same Night – Same Time

"Michael, what are you doing out here at this time of night?" It was Jonetta's soft, sweet voice.

My back was towards her, and it was dark. She could not see the shotgun, so I slowly lowered it down from my chin, but she flipped on the lights and saw the stock of the gun.

"Oh, I was just looking at this old gun." Tears were streaming down my face as I felt her hands slide around my mid-section. She squeezed me tight.

"Michael John," she whispered in my ear. "Why do you have that gun out of the case?" Her voice cracked as she fought back the tears. She knew. She knew me better than anyone in the world.

I was Michael, and I was John... Michael John Shank. John is my middle name and Rose is Jonetta's middle name.

My two names came to represent the two torn halves of myself: Michael, a young, immature Christian whose discouragement with his faith caused him to spiral into unfaithfulness; John, the old man of sin resurrected during Michael's discouragement. Michael spiraled back into sin and John represented Michael's life of sin and unfaithfulness.

"Jonetta Rose," I said. My voice brimmed with shame and guilt. "I am not worthy of you or these children that you've given me."

"Michael?" Jonetta was still squeezing me from behind.

"Yes?" I replied.

"You *are* worthy. It's time to come back to God."

"Jonetta, I can't."

"Why?" she questioned.

"Because I am a worthless, disgusting excuse for a human being–"

"Don't say that!" she interrupted.

"It's true, Jonetta. God will never forgive me for all that I've done," I said as I began to weep.

"Michael, listen to me for just a moment, okay?"

I couldn't speak.

"You know the Bible better than I do, but let me remind you of something."

"What?" I managed to get out.

"David," She said.

"Who?"

"King David. Your sins do not equal David's sins, and God forgave *him*. And do you remember at what moment God forgave him?"

"No." I couldn't believe her strength and ability to encourage such a wretched evil husband.

Jonetta answered her own question, "When David said, '*I've sinned against the Lord.*' Do you remember Nathan's reply?"

"No," I said weakly.

"Nathan said, 'The Lord has put away your sins and you won't die [2 Samuel 12:13]. Michael, God can and *will* forgive you. You've just got to admit your sins and repent of them. The Bible says that if we say we don't have sins, we deceive ourselves–"

"And the Truth is not in us [1 John 1:8]," I interrupted.

"That's right! And the Bible says that if we confess our sins, he is faithful to forgive us of *all* of our unrighteousness" [1 John 1:9].

It was the first glimmer of spiritual hope I had experienced in twelve years. The realization and remembrance of God's love and grace filled my heart. I knelt down to the floor of the garage.

Jonetta had quoted Scripture, and it was the Holy Spirit, through the Scriptures, that convicted my heart of my sins. The Word was amazingly quick and powerful in how it seemed to penetrate my soul and search my disgusting heart [Hebrews 4:12].

We wept together, and she prayed. Yes, my wife prayed for me. Thank God for *good* women!

"Jonetta, I'm so very sorry." Our eyes were swollen and our noses were running. She grabbed a shop-towel, wiped her nose and said, "Michael, I am so sorry, too. Now, wipe your eyes and let me get you something to eat."

As we walked from the garage into the large kitchen I said, "The Camry is gone."

"I know," she replied as she opened the refrigerator door. "That's what woke me up."

My mind began to race as I sat on the kitchen barstool. *If the Camry had not been repossessed, she wouldn't have wakened. If she wouldn't have wakened, she wouldn't have come downstairs to look for me. If she hadn't come downstairs, I would be dead right now and she and the kids would be left with the horrible aftermath. The repo-guys woke her up! She saved my life – our lives.*

"Michael, eat this." She'd put a plate of warmed-up meatloaf in front of me, along with a slice of Red Velvet cake.

"And tomorrow morning we'll decide where we're going to attend Sunday services."

She kissed my cheek, gave me a "side-hug," and went off toward the bedroom.

"Michael," she got my attention before getting out of sight.

"Yeah?" I looked up.

"The man I married would never hurt himself or his family intentionally. So I know I don't have to worry about you tonight, right?"

"Jonetta, you've got nothing to worry about."

She offered that classic gentle smile that I loved so much as she walked down the hall toward the bedroom.

John, that old man of sin, would be hard to kill, but if I didn't kill him he would kill me.

I had met him at the age of thirteen while looking at a legs in Social Studies, then realizing that I was lusting in my heart. It was, at that moment, when I knew that my thoughts were wrong. I had committed sin.

John, that old man of sin, had been buried when I was baptized into Jesus Christ [Colossians 2:11-13].

How had John been resurrected? I did it. I had resurrected John in the midst of discouragement. Discouragement had been the resurrecting power in bringing John back to life, and I was his sole accomplice.

John had grown strong over the past few years, but his strength was limited by *my* permission. It was *my* lust, pride, ego, and selfishness that gave John life, and it was time to dismantle him… one difficult piece at a time.

John wouldn't die without a fight.

Chapter 15

Sharper Than a
Two-Edged Sword

Same Place – Same Night

Where is my Bible? It was 3:30am, but I couldn't sleep. Jonetta's words just a few hours earlier had penetrated my heart. *God's* Word had penetrated my heart.

I went upstairs to our in-home office and rifled through the volumes of books on my office shelves. The shame and guilt mounted, as I realized that I couldn't even find my own Bible.

There it is! I pulled it out. It was tightly wedged between *The Old Man and the Sea* and Donald Fuller's *Applied Anatomy and Physiology for Speech-Language Pathology and Audiology.*

It felt good in my hands – the leather-bound King James Version given to me by Randall.

"How long has it been since I've opened this Bible? Mike, it takes muscle and a shovel. Dig!" I told myself.

"Yeah, but what do you do when your shovel breaks?" I wondered.

"Michael, God will disappoint you again," John whispered in the back of my mind.

I dropped to my knees and brought my hands together in prayer. It had been years since I had prayed on my knees and the feeling was almost embarrassing.

"Dear Father," I prayed softly. "You know *everything* I've done. It's probably not possible for You to forgive me. I... uh (the words weren't coming), well, could You... just... I'm sorry. In Jesus name, Amen." It was a poor attempt at prayer.

It took a long time to find the story of David, but the eight-minute search was fruitful. 2 Samuel 11,

> *And it came to pass in an evening tide, that*
> *David arose from off his bed, and walked upon*
> *the roof of the king's house: and from the roof he*
> *saw a woman washing herself; and the woman*
> *was very beautiful to look upon.*
>
> *And David sent and enquired after the woman.*
> *And one said, Is not this Bathsheba, the*
> *daughter of Eliam, the wife of Uriah the Hittite?*
>
> *And David sent messengers, and took her; and*
> *she came in unto him, and he lay with her; for*
> *she was purified from her uncleanness: and she*
> *returned unto her house.*

And the woman conceived, and sent and told
David, and said, I am with child. And David sent
to Joab, saying, Send me Uriah the Hittite. And
Joab sent Uriah to David.

And when Uriah was come unto him, David
demanded of him how Joab did, and how the
people did, and how the war prospered. And
David said to Uriah, Go down to thy house, and
wash thy feet. And Uriah departed out of the
king's house, and there followed him a mess of
meat from the king.

But Uriah slept at the door of the king's house
with all the servants of his lord, and went not
down to his house. And when they had told
David, saying, Uriah went not down unto his
house, David said unto Uriah, Camest thou not
from thy journey? Why then didst thou not go
down unto thine house? And Uriah said unto
David, The ark, and Israel, and Judah, abide in
tents; and my lord Joab, and the servants of my
lord, are encamped in the open fields; shall I

*then go into mine house, to eat and to drink, and
to lie with my wife? As thou livest, and as thy
soul liveth, I will not do this thing. And David
said to Uriah, Tarry here today also, and
tomorrow I will let thee depart.*

*So Uriah abode in Jerusalem that day, and the
morrow. And when David had called him, he did
eat and drink before him; and he made him
drunk: and at even he went out to lie on his bed
with the servants of his lord, but went not down
to his house.*

*And it came to pass in the morning, that David
wrote a letter to Joab, and sent it by the hand of
Uriah. And he wrote in the letter, saying, Set ye
Uriah in the forefront of the hottest battle, and
retire ye from him, that he may be smitten, and
die.*

*And it came to pass, when Joab observed the
city that he assigned Uriah unto a place where
he knew that valiant men were. And the men of*

*the city went out, and fought with Joab: and
there fell some of the people of the servants of
David; and Uriah the Hittite died also.*

*Then Joab sent and told David all the things
concerning the war; And charged the
messenger, saying, When thou hast made an end
of telling the matters of the war unto the king,
And if so be that the king's wrath arise, and he
say unto thee, Wherefore approached ye so nigh
unto the city when ye did fight? Knew ye not that
they would shoot from the wall? Who smote
Abimelech the son of Jerubbesheth? Did not a
woman cast a piece of a millstone upon him
from the wall that he died in Thebez? Why went
ye nigh the wall?*

*Then say thou, Thy servant Uriah the Hittite is
dead also. So the messenger went, and came
and shewed David all that Joab had sent him
for. And the messenger said unto David, Surely
the men prevailed against us, and came out unto
us into the field, and we were upon them even*

unto the entering of the gate. And the shooters shot from off the wall upon thy servants; and some of the king's servants be dead, and thy servant Uriah the Hittite is dead also.

Then David said unto the messenger, Thus shalt thou say unto Joab, Let not this thing displease thee, for the sword devoureth one as well as another: make thy battle more strong against the city, and overthrow it: and encourage thou him.

And when the wife of Uriah heard that Uriah her husband was dead, she mourned for her husband. And when the mourning was past, David sent and fetched her to his house, and she became his wife, and bare him a son.

But the thing that David had done displeased the LORD (2 Samuel 11:2-27, KJV).

Even after reading through the account of David's sins with Bathsheba, I felt no better. My sins were greater than David's, weren't they?

Men tend to compare themselves to other men. It's what we do. Paul warned against this, saying,

For we dare not make ourselves of the number, or compare ourselves with some that commend themselves: but they measuring themselves by themselves, and comparing themselves among themselves, are not wise (2 Corinthians 10:12).

Even though Paul said that we're not wise if we compare ourselves to others, I couldn't help pulling out the pad of paper and an ink pen.

I have to know if my sins are greater than David's sins. I listed David's sins in a numerical order, studying each verse of the text.

1. Lust of the eyes and flesh (v.2)
2. Yielding to lust via pursuit (v.3)
3. Abuse of power (v.4)
4. Kidnapping and potential rape (v.4)
5. Illegitimate pregnancy (v.5)
6. Corrupt motive in contacting her husband (v.6)
7. Surreptitious counseling with an ulterior motive (v.7)

8. Abuse of power repeated; a command with an ulterior motive; a secretive desire for Uriah to sleep with his wife, thereby establishing an alibi for the illegitimate pregnancy by David (v.8)

9. Bribery with gifts/rewards (meat from the king) (v.8)

10. David's lack of conviction, friendship, loyalty: David's conscience was still unaffected by Uriah's loyalty in "sleeping at the door of the King's house" when Uriah would have certainly desired to spend a single night with his loving wife and in the comfort of his own bed (v.9)

11. David's lack of human empathy (v.9)

12. David's lack of brotherly compassion: David had illegitimate sex with his loyal commander's wife, and yet his commander, Uriah, chose to sleep in discomfort at David's doorstep, showing undying loyalty and respect to David, his Commander and Chief, unselfishly denying himself of his own masculine desires to be with his wife (v.9)

13. David's corruption: David's premeditated plan didn't work, so he sought to find answers to establish another plan (v.10)

14. David's denial of righteousness: Uriah's righteousness, love, and loyalty was presented and deflected (vs. 11-12)

15. David's abuse of power: David uses his power and influence, commanding Uriah to stay in Jerusalem so that David could revise his plan (v.12)

16. David fostered drunkenness toward the success of his own corrupt agenda (v.13)

17. David's rejection of the will of God: David deflected, again, the righteousness of Uriah when Uriah demonstrated his own loyalty, love, and uprightness toward David (v.13)

18. David schemes premeditated murder: David writes the plan of the murder of Uriah (v.14)

19. David commits the ultimate betrayal: A plan for the murder of a man, delivered by the hands of the victim (v.15)

20. David's written admission of his sinful plan (v.15)

21. David's corrupt plan of murder, phase 1: (v.16)

22. The loss of many lives for the success of David's cover-up, phase 2 (v.17)

23. David's murder-plan successful, phase 3 (v.17)

24. David's marginalizing/dismissing of his own corruption (vv. 18-25)

25. David's encouragement toward the continued cover-up (vv. 18-25)

26. Consuming the widow's house (v.26; Matthew 23:14; Luke 20:47)

I then listed my own sins:

1. Disbelief

2. Discouragement

3. Discontinuing prayer

4. Forsaking the assembly

5. Forsaking partaking of the Lord's supper

6. Bringing reproach upon the name of the Lord

7. Bringing reproach upon the church

8. Soiling my name and character in the community

9. Forsaking the Word

10. Quenching the Spirit

11. Willful sin

12. Lying

13. Hatefulness

14. Worldliness

15. Sexual immorality

16. Neglect of my wife

17. Neglect of my children

18. Allowing the cares of the world to choke out the Word

19. Bitterness

20. Wrath

21. Violence

22. Betrayal

23. Illicit drug use

24. Drunkenness

25. Filth of every kind

26. Desire for ill-gotten gain

Could someone previously baptized into Jesus Christ for the remission of sins be forgiven of a list of sins like *this*? I didn't think so. It still looked to me like David's sins were not as bad as mine.

In my mind, there was no hope left. Job said, "*My days are swifter than a weaver's shuttle, and are spent without hope*" (Job 7:6).

Maybe I should have just pulled that trigger. My family would have had the insurance money. My children would have been provided for, and the world would be a better place.

God had a different idea...

Chapter 16
Dangerous Expectations
The Downward Spiritual Spiral

No one decides to leave the Lord overnight.
Leaving the Lord usually happens in small, incremental
steps.

Every man and woman, young or old, who makes
the decision to obey the gospel is initially excited, zealous,
and eager to make the commitment to surrender their life to
Jesus Christ. They are typically enthusiastic about sharing
their new faith with those that they love. So what causes
some to remain faithful unto death (Revelation 2:10) and
others to fall away (Revelation 2:4-5)?

The question is far too complex, with as many
variables as there are people. However, it seemed in *our*
case that it came down to expectations, more specifically,
unbiblical expectations.

I had made the monumental mistake in thinking that
the Christian life would be a life free from difficulties,
problems, and struggles. How would any honest, rational,
intelligent person develop this incorrect expectation? The
answer was as clear as the nose on my face – *I'd never
heard any member of the Lord's church talk about their
own struggles, temptations, or sins in their life.*

It truly appeared to me that everyone in the Lord's
church was perfect. They were perfect people, perfectly

dressed, perfect in their speech and behavior, and were living the perfect life. As my friend Chris put it, it's almost a country-club atmosphere, and there was a self-inflicted pressure to fit in.

Oh sure, I'd heard plenty of sermons on struggle, disappointment, temptation and sin. That is a given. But individual Christians simply did not admit or discuss *their own* sins.

Some were quick to discuss other people's sins by gossiping, which is a cancer in the church, but they didn't talk about their own problems, even though God encourages us to do so (James 5:16; 1 John 1:9).

And why won't Christians admit their own sins and discuss their own faults with others in the church? The fear of judgment and the fear of further gossip.

It is a genuine fear to think that someone in the church would judge you as *unfaithful*. And if you're branded as unfaithful, it is a difficult thing to overcome.

Fear of judgment by brothers and sisters in Christ was the first barrier. And the second barrier? Gossip.

Look, if Christians gossip about everyone else's sins, what will these people say about *me* and *my* sins to others? Would I honestly want to take the risk of confessing my sins to these people, even though the Lord instructs me to do so?

I had observed some gossip during my "faithful" years, and it scared me. Some in the brotherhood *perceived* themselves to be more righteous than others, and a telling sign was their tongue: gossiping, maligning, backbiting and disparaging other struggling Christians. It made me sick.

Self-righteous brethren took advantage of every opportunity to "discuss" the faults of others; however, their defense cry was, "I'm only telling the truth!"

In addition, my expectations were wrong. I wanted that "perfect life" that I *thought* all other Christians enjoyed. When life became less than perfect, I became disappointed in God. Disappointment led to discouragement. Discouragement led me to neglect the Word and prayer. The neglect of God's Word and regular communication with Him caused spiritual starvation.

The Word of God is the essential food for the life of one's soul. It is living water (John 4:10, 14), milk (1 Peter 2:2), bread (John 6:33), strong meat (Hebrews 5:12), and sweeter than honey (Psalm 119:103).

The soul starves without it, and when something starves long enough, it dies. When our faith dies, reverting to our old selves and our old ways is an easy transition. It is the default mode.

In my case, I was far worse than before I'd known the Truth. It reminded me of Christ's words,

> *When the unclean spirit is gone out of a man, he walketh through dry places, seeking rest, and findeth none. Then he saith, I will return into my house from whence I came out; and when he is come, he findeth it empty, swept, and garnished. Then goeth he, and taketh with himself seven other spirits more wicked than himself, and they enter in and dwell there: and the last state of that man is worse than the first. Even so shall it be also unto this wicked generation* (Matthew 12:43-45).

> *For if after they have escaped the pollutions of the world through the knowledge of the Lord and Saviour Jesus Christ, they are again entangled therein, and overcome, the*

latter end is worse with them than the

beginning. For it had been better for them

not to have known the way of righteousness,

than, after they have known it, to turn from

the holy commandment delivered unto them.

But it is happened unto them according to

the true proverb, the dog is turned to his own

vomit again; and the sow that was washed to

her wallowing in the mire (2 Peter 2:20-22).

Unbiblical expectations. Disappointment. Discouragement. Discontinued study and prayer. Spiritual starvation. Spiritual death. Resurrection of the old man of sin.

Chapter 17
Not Even a
Thank You Wave

August, 2004: Lake Dallas, Texas

The following Sunday we found a church of Christ close by and attended services. It was a large congregation, and I was uncomfortable.

The morning service started with the announcements of happenings in the church, then another man stepped behind the podium and began leading the singing.

"Not one person has said hello to us," I whispered to Jonetta. She shook her head in the affirmative and continued singing.

"Do you not find that weird?" I asked through another whisper.

She shook her head yes while she sang. How'd she do it? How could anyone multi-task like she did? I could barely walk and chew gum at the same time, much less try to have and conversation *and sing* at the same time!

Andrew and Paul, now fourteen and ten, sang about the way boys who are that age try to sing – moving their lips with almost no sound coming out. Noah, now four years old, sang louder than anyone. He seemed "at home" in the crowd, while Lane, three months old, slept soundly in Jonetta's arms.

The minister's sermon droned on. I looked at the boys and they were predictably bored.

"Paul," I bumped his side with a whisper. "Wake up!" He snapped awake and sat up.

The last song closed and people started to mill out of the building. We smiled at those around us and tried to speak to several.

"Is it just me, or is that place filled with a bunch of unfriendly robots?" I quipped as we pulled out of the church parking lot. I waved an old couple to go ahead and pull out in front of us, trying to be the "courteous Christian." The woman driving looked at us with a pursed, unpleasant look. Then she slowly pulled out in front of us – not even a "thank you" wave.

"See – see what I'm talking about!" I blurted to Jonetta in a hushed tone. "Here we are, trying to come back to the Lord, and we have to deal with this kind of attitude–"

"Honey," she tried to calm the situation, "it's the first Sunday. Let's give it a chance."

"Yeah," I said in the same hushed tone, "I'd like to give these old people in front of us the bird! Who doesn't give the mandatory 'thank you' wave when someone lets you out in this kind of traffic?"

"Michael, what are we going to do for lunch?" She changed the subject. We had no money, literally *no* money left. And almost no groceries left. Our $1,700.00/month rent was two months behind, and we had about $100.00 in our checking account. And our savings account? Yeah, that was a joke.

"I've got $200.00 in petty cash at the office. If we get that, can we stop at Kroger?"

"That'd be great," she replied. "I'll make us a good lunch then we'll make a grocery run. Is that okay?" she asked. My shame mounted, but my appreciation for her love, attitude, and support had never been greater.

"I love you." It was all I could say.

"I love you, too," she replied.

Jonetta busied herself with making lunch. Noah was on the counter helping her, and Lane was sleeping in the baby-swing. The older boys were in the living room playing a video game, so I took advantage of the time and called my brother in law...

"So Mitchell" I said into the phone, "I know you've been wanting to buy those two Honda Recons that we have

in the barn at Jonetta's parents. How much will you give
me for them?"

Chapter 18
Texas Cockleburs
August, 2004: Lake Dallas, Texas

Mitchell had agreed to $3,200.00 for the pair of Honda ATV's – that'd be almost enough to get us close to being caught up on our residential lease. I squeezed another $600.00 out of the business, which gave us a little gas, grocery, and operating money for the week.

The stress of being completely broke was beyond description, and the fact that I'd laid off the last of my employees made our future hopeless.

"I don't know how, but we're going to be okay," Jonetta encouraged me as I stood in the dark of the back yard, smoking a cigarette.

"Jonetta," I started without looking at her, "I'm so ashamed of all that I've done – my sins, my mistakes, my horrible decisions. I just want you to know that I'm ready to try again. I want to live the life that God wants me to live, but I'm scared," I said as I flipped the cigarette across the yard.

"What are you scared of?" she asked as she stepped closer to me – "Oh, oh, oh, oh!" Jonetta was hopping on one foot while pulling the other foot up close to her waist with her hands.

"Don't move – don't move!" I raised my voice. She'd stepped on one of those little cocklebur things that grow in Texas grass. What are those things, anyway?

We cautiously moved to the concrete back patio after a careful removal of the Texas-lawn-cocklebur thingy and resumed our talk.

"I'm scared of failing again," I admitted.

"Failing what again?" Jonetta asked.

"Failing God," I said. "I'm scared that I can't repent, and I also don't want God to think that I'm coming back to him just because we're in need."

"You need to think about the Prodigal Son, Michael."

She was a wise woman.

I stood there waiting on her to continue.

"Maybe God has been waiting on you to spend your metaphorical inheritance and hit rock bottom. Maybe this is exactly what you've needed to realize your need for Him," she said with love and logic. "Men like you – men who are driven, ambitious, and hard-headed – are hard to manage.

"And men like you, men who have zeal and a strong will should *use* that zeal for good, not for bad. Yeah, you've went down the wrong road, but you *can* change your course."

"Is it that simple to you, Jonetta? Is it just a decision away?" I asked without any sarcasm.

"Michael," she turned toward the patio door. "Let me get a band aid for my foot, then I want to show you something."

I followed her through the door. While she went to the kitchen to get a band aid, I went to the restroom. After returning to the kitchen I saw her sitting at the island with her Bible.

"Come here, honey," she said while holding her finger in the book. I sat down next to her.

"Read these verses."

I read,

> *I call heaven and earth to record this day against you, that I have set before you life and death, blessing and cursing:* ***therefore choose life, that both thou and thy seed may live****: That thou mayest love the LORD thy God, and that thou mayest obey his voice, and that thou mayest cleave unto him: for he is thy life, and the length of thy*

*days: that thou mayest dwell in the land
which the LORD sware unto thy fathers, to
Abraham, to Isaac, and to Jacob, to give
them* (Deuteronomy 30:19-20).

There was so much of the Bible that I'd forgotten over the years. Use it or lose it, right?

"Michael," she said, "you asked me if it was just a decision away. It says here in verse 19 to choose life so that you and your seed may live. And that you may love Him, obey Him, and cleave to Him."

I looked up at her.

"It *is* just a decision away," Jonetta said.

"The prodigal made that decision," I said looking back at her Bible.

"You want to find out?"

"Yes."

She flipped to the New Testament, Luke 15. "Do you want to read it out loud?" she asked.

"No," I hesitated. "You go ahead." Even though I was the man of the house, Jonetta was the one leading us back to the Lord. If she was willing to help me back to God, I certainly didn't find fault in her reading the Bible out loud.

She read, starting in verse 11,

And he said, A certain man had two sons:
And the younger of them said to his father,
Father, give me the portion of goods that
falleth to me. And he divided unto them his
living.

And not many days after the younger son
gathered all together, and took his journey
into a far country, and there wasted his
substance with riotous living. And when
he had spent all, there arose a mighty
famine in that land; and he began to be in
want. And he went and joined himself to a
citizen of that country; and he sent him
into his fields to feed swine. And he would
fain have filled his belly with the husks that
the swine did eat: and no man gave unto
him.

And when he came to himself, he said,
How many hired servants of my father's
have bread enough and to spare, and I

perish with hunger! I will arise and go to my father, and will say unto him, Father, I have sinned against heaven, and before thee, and am no more worthy to be called thy son: make me as one of thy hired servants. And he arose, and came to his father.

But when he was yet a great way off, his father saw him, and had compassion, and ran, and fell on his neck, and kissed him. And the son said unto him, Father, I have sinned against heaven, and in thy sight, and am no more worthy to be called thy son. But the father said to his servants, Bring forth the best robe, and put it on him; and put a ring on his hand, and shoes on his feet: and bring hither the fatted calf, and kill it; and let us eat, and be merry: for this my son was dead, and is alive again; he was lost, and is found. And they began to be merry.

Now his elder son was in the field: and as he came and drew nigh to the house, he heard music and dancing. And he called one of the servants, and asked what these things meant. And he said unto him, Thy brother is come; and thy father hath killed the fatted calf, because he hath received him safe and sound. And he was angry, and would not go in: therefore came his father out, and entreated him. And he answering said to his father, Lo, these many years do I serve thee, neither transgressed I at any time thy commandment: and yet thou never gavest me a kid, that I might make merry with my friends: But as soon as this thy son was come, which hath devoured thy living with harlots, thou hast killed for him the fatted calf.

And he said unto him, Son, thou art ever with me, and all that I have is thine. It was meet that we should make merry, and be

> *glad: for this thy brother was dead, and is*
> *alive again; and was lost, and is found.*
> (Luke 15:11-32).

Tears started to well up in my eyes; it was uncontrollable. The Word was doing its job on my mind and heart.

"Michael, this was a son. He left his father and the joys of his father's home to live a riotous, sinful life. He became broke and found himself at rock-bottom.

"And look at what it says here, '*He came to himself.*' He came to his senses and realized the person he'd become, so he went back to his father, thinking he'd be nothing more than a hired servant.

"Look at what happened when he came back to his father and admitted that he had sinned. His father restored him! Michael, the man's father rejoiced when he saw him coming back from afar off!"

I began to laugh through the tears. It was a laughter of deep relief and joy and excitement! I grabbed Jonetta and hugged her tight.

"It really is possible, isn't it?" I asked through tears.

"Michael, it is God's plan. He doesn't want anybody to perish, but everyone to repent" (2 Peter 3:9). She squeezed me tightly.

Small rays of hope started to appear. It had been a long time.

Chapter 19
Use a Little Deodorant
September 2004: Lake Dallas, Texas

And as Jesus passed forth from thence, he saw a man, named Matthew, sitting at the receipt of custom: and he saith unto him, Follow me. And he arose, and followed him. And it came to pass, as Jesus sat at meat in the house, behold, many publicans and sinners came and sat down with him and his disciples. And when the Pharisees saw it, they said unto his disciples, Why eateth your Master with publicans and sinners? But when Jesus heard that, he said unto them, They that be whole need not a physician, but they that are sick. But go ye and learn what that meaneth, I will have mercy, and not sacrifice: for I am not come to call the righteous, but sinners to repentance.

Matthew 9:11-13

It was the end of September, 2004. We had been attending the local church for about for 6 weeks. My drinking had diminished and I had been reading the Bible. Jonetta's constant encouragement had been a source of strength.

"Honey, do you not find it strange that the preacher hasn't contacted us?" I was parked on the couch holding Lane. We had him wrapped up in a little cotton blanket cocoon. The older boys had taken Noah down to the subdivision's swimming pool, and Jonetta was sitting in the over-sized chair across from the couch.

"Yeah, it is a little weird." She admitted. "I've filled out several visitor cards with our contact information and put 'em in the plate." Visitor cards are little paper cards usually found in the pew-backs of every church. The procedure is pretty much the same around the country: visitors to the church pull out the card, fill in all of the information with a sawed-off pencil, and drop them into the collection plate.

"Do they have so many visitors that they can't get to them all?" I asked.

"Maybe so," she said without any emotion. Jonetta needed help in bringing me back, and her desperation was evident.

"Maybe if you'd use a little deodorant, the preacher would stop by–"

"Shut up you idiot!" she shot back. I threw a couch-pillow at her, but she deflected it across the room. Teasing her was always fun.

"Hey, maybe if we sit close to the front and holler an 'Amen' every few seconds, someone will notice." I said with a laugh.

"Michael, stop it," she said… but she laughed.

"Jonetta, seriously, we've attended this congregation for over a month and we've not made a single friend – and that's *not* because we haven't tried."

"Yeah, you're right, but let's not make our faith about them. Let's just keep doing what's right."

"How about we try another congregation?" I asked.

"Where do we go?" She seemed open to the idea.

"Wait a minute–" I interrupted.

"What's wrong?"

I stood up and handed the baby to Jonetta. "I think he's pooped–"

"Oh, thanks a lot!" She took him from my arms.

"Let me grab the phone book. There's got to be another church of Christ in our area."

The next Sunday morning we pulled into the parking lot of a large congregation north of Lake Dallas. The boys jumped out of the back, and Jonetta pulled Lane from the baby carrier.

"Hello!" came a voice from somewhere.

"Uh, hello!" I said to a young couple that had hollered at us from a few cars down. The guy approached us with his hand extended and a big smile.

"I'm Grant, and this is my wife, Emily," he greeted us as if we were the POTUS and wife. When I shook Grant's hand, I noticed that his shirt was from Land's End... his initials were embroidered on the cuff. Why notice something like that? Who knows?

"I'm Mike, and this is my wife Jonetta," happily returning the greeting.

"Are you folks visiting with us today?" He'd had a lot of coffee.

"Yes, we are. This is our first time here," I said with a smile. Wow, this was nice.

"That's great! How about me and Emily introduce you to some of the brothers and sisters here?"

I looked at Jonetta and she looked at me.

"That'd be great," I replied.

Grant and Emily were real people. Come to find out, he was an engineer and she worked as a dental hygienist. We "clicked" immediately.

The brethren seemed to be so happy that we were there. They talked to the boys, doted over the baby, and were concerned about making sure that we felt "at home."

A sweet young girl took our older boys to a Bible class, and we followed Grant and Emily to the young adult's class.

"Hey, we have another new couple visiting with us today," Grant announced to the class. "Michael and Jonetta… I forgot their last names." He confessed, and everyone laughed. They found us chairs and pulled another couple of chairs close to us.

Love and acceptance is an important ingredient in the healing and edifying of the weak, even when you are unaware of the need.

Wherefore receive ye one another, as Christ also received us to the glory of God (Romans 15:7).

Chapter 20

Burying John…
The Second Time

November 2004: Lake Dallas, Texas

I have heard hundreds of brethren make the statement, "We do not attend church services to be entertained." We are there to offer the one Creator of the universe our sincerest, most heart-felt worship, according to His perfect will.

Jesus told the woman at the well,

> *Jesus saith unto her, Woman, believe me, the hour cometh, when ye shall neither in this mountain, nor yet at Jerusalem, worship the Father. Ye worship ye know not what: we know what we worship: for salvation is of the Jews. But the hour cometh, and now is, when the true worshippers shall worship the Father in spirit and in truth: for the Father seeketh such to worship him* (John 4:21-23).

Our God seeks those who will worship Him in spirit and in Truth. At the same time, there is an unspoken question not asked within the heart of the masses: is proper worship to God intended to be ritualistic and boring?

If you pine for a liturgical type of worship, then ritualistic and boring is your thing. However, New

Testament worship that is patterned after the ancient first century church should be *anything* but boring!

The preaching at this particular congregation north of Lake Dallas congregation was passionate and exciting. It wasn't new or "liberal." It was simply delivered with a raw candor and an excitement that I hadn't heard in a long time. It reminded me of some of the old recordings of Marshall Keeble's sermons that I had heard.

The singing was exuberant, and the prayers weren't repetitions of "trained speeches," but rather were prayers humbly expressed from the prayer leader's heart.

The services were not liberal or conservative, but biblical. They were as close to any New Testament practice as I had ever seen.

We, as a family, had been attending this congregation over the past five weeks and we felt refreshed. It was the middle of November, 2004. As we sat and listened to today's lesson, the Word penetrated both joint and marrow.

The assembly stood as they began the last song. It was the song of encouragement for those who might become Christians and those would be restored.

During the first verse, Jonetta bumped my arm. I looked over and she had her Bible open, pointing to a verse – it was Luke 15:10, the verse right before the Prodigal Son,

> *Likewise, I say unto you, there is joy in the presence of the angels of God over one sinner that repenteth.*

It was the encouragement I needed. I stepped out of the pew and walked up the aisle. The need to repent and confess my sins before the church was heavier than an elephant sitting on a porch swing.

The minister smiled, took my hand, and we sat down together on the front pew. We talked about what I needed to do.

When the song was finished, he stood and addressed the church, explaining that I had been unfaithful for many years, but desired repentance and forgiveness.

"Michael would like to say a few words." He looked down at me. A nervous knot in my stomach seemed to rise toward into my throat.

Ahem-ahem (I tried to clear the lump in my throat). My voice quivered,

"My name is Michael Shank. While we're not actually members of this congregation. I've come forward to. . . (*Ahem*)... ask you to pray for me. I have committed terrible sins against God, my wife, my family... in public. Uh... I am ashamed to admit that suicide seemed to be the only answer a few weeks ago."

The crowd gasped.

"I want to repent and hope that God can forgive me... I, uh, well, we're not sure where to go from here. All we ask is that you might pray for us."

The response from the brethren was truly incredible. Men hugged me, women wept on my shoulder, the elders gathered around us and led a prayer. People slipped us little paper notes of encouragement. Some contained verses of encouragement. People kissed our boys and hugged Jonetta. The Deacons surrounded us and begged us to let them help us. God's love and grace was demonstrated through these wonderful brethren.

John was, once again, buried. I prayed that he would stay in that hole and that I would never let discouragement, or anything else, bring him back to life.

Chapter 21
The Envelope
December 2004: Lake Dallas, Texas

For I have known the thoughts that I am thinking towards you--an affirmation of Jehovah; **thoughts of peace, and not of evil, to give to you posterity and hope.**

Jeremiah 29:11

December, 2004:

We had flourished in the congregation north of Lake Dallas. Many friendships were developed and we became active once again in that local body of Jesus Christ (Acts 20:28).

My business continued its down-hill slide into the abyss, but my spiritual life had *never* been better!

One evening at our mid-week Bible study I confessed to Grant that I didn't have the money to buy Christmas gifts for our children.

"Brother, let me help you," he pled.

"No, no, Grant. That's not why I'm sharing this with you. I'm only asking for you to pray for us. I'm so worried that the kids won't have any gifts this year. We didn't celebrate Christmas as a "religious" holiday, but we enjoyed the tradition of gift-giving, family, and the fellowship that goes with that time of the year.

"Let's pray right now, Michael."

Grant prayed fervently. I wondered if and how would God answer his prayer?

It was Thursday night, December 23rd. Jonetta answered the door, but no one was there. She stepped outside into the cool December air to look around. There, under the doorbell, was an envelope. She brought it inside and showed it to me. The boys had heard the doorbell and started filing down the stairs.

"Who is it, Mom?" Andrew asked.

"I don't know; someone just left this envelope," she said.

"Can I open it?" asked Paul.

"Open it, Paul," I encouraged him.

The plain white envelope had two words written neatly in ink across the front,

Shank Family

We all gathered around Paul as he peeled up the flap. Inside was $963.00 in cash and a note, "God loves you."

Someone from the church. We couldn't believe it! God had answered Grant's prayer! Thanks be to God! Our children were affected the most.

"Dad," Andrew said, "Maybe we should give a little of *this* to some poor people." We *were* the poor people, but our boys didn't know. And their concern? Other poor people. It's a great day in life when your own kids get it!

"Andrew, that's an excellent idea!" We rejoiced and thanked God repeatedly.

God works *through* people. He doesn't drop the answers to our needs from the sky. He doesn't manipulate us like puppets on a string. He doesn't infringe upon our free will.

He does, however, work *through* people. We see this idea repeated throughout the Scriptures. When Jesus struck down Saul of Tarsus, speaking to him in a one-on-one dialogue, Jesus could have easily answered Saul's direct question with a direct answer, but He didn't. Christ took the opportunity to direct Saul *through another person*, Ananias.

> *And as he journeyed, he came near Damascus: and suddenly there shined round about him a light from heaven: And he fell to the earth, and heard a voice saying unto him, Saul, Saul, why persecutest thou me? And he said, Who art thou, Lord? And the Lord said, I am Jesus whom thou persecutest: it is hard for thee to kick against the pricks. And he trembling and astonished said, **Lord, what***

> ***wilt thou have me to do?*** *And the Lord*
> *said unto him, Arise, and go into the city,*
> *and **it shall be told thee what thou must do***
> (Acts 9:3-6).

> *And Ananias went his way, and entered*
> *into the house; and putting his hands on*
> *him said, Brother Saul, the Lord, even*
> *Jesus, that appeared unto thee in the way*
> *as thou camest, hath sent me, that thou*
> *mightest receive thy sight, and be filled*
> *with the Holy Ghost. And immediately*
> *there fell from his eyes as it had been*
> *scales: and he received sight forthwith,*
> *and arose, and was baptized* (Acts 9:17-
> 18).

Jesus intervened in the lives of two men: Saul and
Ananias. He used Ananias as His mouth-piece, rather
than telling Saul what to do Himself.

While we don't find that Ananias "told him what he
must do" in Acts 9:17-18, we do find it in Paul's
salvation testimonial in Acts 22. This is an example of
the need to study the entire context rather than one small

section of Scripture. Acts 22 says,

> *And one Ananias, a devout man according*
>
> *to the law, having a good report of all the*
>
> *Jews which dwelt there, Came unto me,*
>
> *and stood, and said unto me, Brother Saul,*
>
> *receive thy sight. And the same hour I*
>
> *looked up upon him. And he said, The God*
>
> *of our fathers hath chosen thee, that thou*
>
> *shouldest know his will, and see that Just*
>
> *One, and shouldest hear the voice of his*
>
> *mouth. For thou shalt be his witness unto*
>
> *all men of what thou hast seen and heard.*
>
> *And now why tarriest thou? Arise, and be*
>
> *baptized, and wash away thy sins, calling*
>
> *on the name of the Lord* (Acts 22:12-16).

Jesus commanded Saul, through Ananias, to obey
His will. Christ, using the Holy Spirit working through
Ananias, gave Saul's sight back to him. Christ in the
same manner instructed Saul of his future mission, then
told Saul *what he must do* to wash away his sins.

What's the point? The point is that God still uses
people to accomplish His will today. God used those
good people within the church to answer Grant's prayer.

The Bible and prayer – the corner posts that give our spiritual life the opportunity to be established, to grow, and to have eternal life. Jesus said,

> *Search the scriptures; for in them ye think ye have eternal life: and they are they which testify of me* (John 5:39).

Our spiritual starvation was being reversed. We started to eat again, but our struggles were far from over.

Chapter 22
Living on Luuuuv!
January 2005: Lake Dallas, Texas

January, 2005:

"We should go back home," I suggested. It was early morning, and we laid in bed enjoying the quiet. Lane was sleeping soundly, and the older boys weren't up yet.

"I've been thinking the same thing," Jonetta replied. "But, we'll have the same problem we had when we left."

"Yeah, that's what worries me," I admitted.

"What about the church close to Carterville?" she asked. It was one of the few growing congregations in southern Illinois.

"I can't think of anywhere else, Jonetta."

"And a job?"

"I can renew my Illinois audiology license and try to go to work for another firm," I answered with hesitation.

"Michael," she knew something was wrong, "you don't really want to go back to Audiology, do you?"

"No, but it's one of the few things I know well," I said.

"Well, you know what we need to do, don't you?" she asked.

"Yes. Buy a lottery ticket!" I said with enthusiasm.

"No, goofy! We need to pray," she encouraged.

"How 'bout we do both?" I smiled.

"I'll kill you if you waste a dollar–" she looked serious.

"Just kidding!" I quickly interrupted. "Besides..."

"Besides what?" Jonetta asked.

"We don't *have* a dollar," I said as I put on a pitiful face. She burst out in laughter.

"But," she said in her laughter, "we've got luuuuv!"

"Sometimes," I tried to be serious, "you really know how to kill the romance!"

Chapter 23
The Fatherless
January 2005: Lake Dallas, Texas

The office was lonely the following Monday morning. I had been forced to terminate every staff member's position.

I was busy boxing up files and calling vendors to cancel my accounts.

The quietness of the office was interrupted by the "ding" of front door's alarm. Someone had entered the front door of the office. I walked to the reception area and a young man was standing just inside the door holding something in his hand.

"Can I help you?" I asked with an extended hand.

"I'm Josh and wanted to see if you'd let me hang up this flyer. We're having a gospel meeting in March, just up the street."

"Oh, where do you attend?" Members of the churches of Christ are some of the only ones who use the term "gospel meeting." Denominations typically use the term "Revival."

"I'm a member of the _____ church of Christ." He seemed tense. Maybe it was his first time putting out flyers.

"Fantastic, Brother! We're members at the

_____ congregation, just north of Lake Dallas!" I was

genuinely excited to meet another brother in Christ.

"Oh, yeah, I know that church. Liberals don't

usually attend our meetings," he said nastily as he turned

toward the door.

"Whoa, Josh, wait a minute. What are you talking

about?" I was well aware of the differences between the

conservative congregations and liberal congregations, but

the church we attended was not considered to be a

"liberal" church.

He turned around to face me. "Your church

supports orphanages," He stated flatly.

"Yeah?" My tone was more of a question than an

answer.

"That's unscriptural, and it *proves* you are a liberal."

The guy wanted a fight. It was too bad I hadn't run into

him a few months before.

"So, let me ask *you* a question?" I remained

unusually calm. "How many orphans have your members

adopted?"

"Well, I don't keep count–"

"You must have *some* idea," I encouraged.

"No, I really don't know," he grew more nervous.

"How about just *one*? Has any family at your congregation opened their home to *one* orphan?" I asked. "And be honest."

"Not that I know of–" Josh admitted.

"So," I interrupted, "your belief is that is unscriptural to give money from the contribution to brethren who do the work of supporting and taking care of orphans, but the brethren at the _____ church of Christ have not adopted a single orphan?"

"Look, I don't want to debate–"

"This is not a debate," I again interrupted. "You called me a liberal and I want to know why. You accuse us of doing something unscriptural – which we are not, and you refuse to take any personal responsibility in helping these children–"

"All I know," Josh interrupted, "is that you cannot take money from the contribution and give it to something like an orphanage."

"Well, you are concerned about doing things the Bible way and I respect that. I want the *same* thing," I was fighting to be humble.

"Josh, wait right there just a sec." I went to my briefcase and pulled out my old Bible that I had just begun to carry with me again.

I walked back toward Josh while flipping to the book of James.

"Brother, what about this verse?" I pointed to the verse and asked him to read it out loud. Josh read:

> *Pure religion and undefiled before God and the Father is this, To visit the fatherless and widows in their affliction, and to keep himself unspotted from the world* (James 1:27).

"Josh, how many fatherless children did you visit and care for this past month?" I asked sincerely.

Josh turned toward the door and exited quickly.

Seriously? Did that just happen? I remembered back to my studies with Randall and realized how splintered – how divided – our brotherhood had become. I was so glad that my life was no longer ruled by "John," because John would have slapped that guy up side his head without a second thought.

But it was a blessing in disguise. Josh's attitude and his judgmental statement forced me make a decision... it was time to fix the broken shovel.

Chapter 24
The Head and
The Heart
Polar Extremes

We in the Lord's church are great at talking to the head, but how are we at talking to the heart?

Christ's church battled the false doctrines of the Holiness Movement in the 1930's. We have battled the Apostolic Church of God's false claims of being able to heal the sick in the 1940's. We fought against the Pentecostal's claims of being "slain in the Spirit" and speaking in tongues (spouting gibberish which is clearly not any known language and without an interpreter) from the 1950's until this very day.

The religious world, at this point, has become steeped in blind emotionalism. A premium has been placed on feelings rather than the rational, intelligent teachings of God's Word.

But it was in the 1980's that our own problems appeared. A growing chasm within our brotherhood: those who wanted to embrace more emotionalism and a "wider fellowship" in one corner against those who cautioned against emotionalism with a foundational desire to ask for a *Thus saith the Lord* in all spiritual matters in the other corner.

The internal war within the church of our Lord had begun, and the opposing sides had a polarizing effect; brethren migrated to one corner or the other.

When lines are drawn and sides are chosen, the natural progression for each side is to "dig in" for the long hall.

Even though our brethren recognized this phenomena in the 1920's and had tried to fight it with little success, some of our brethren had now grown tired of being different. They decided that it would be easier to take the road of ecumenicalism, in spite of our Lord's "narrow-mindedness."

Jesus, narrow-minded? Everything about the cause of Christ is narrow-minded. His teaching in Mark 10:2-12 was so narrow-minded that He was ridiculed.

Today's so-called "enlightened" are those who are "overly" open-minded. Hyper-open-mindedness seems to be a type of "virtue" in our contemporary society. However, Peter said that there is not any other name in which salvation is found than Jesus Christ (Acts 4:12). Say that to the world today and you will be castigated.

Jesus was truly narrow-minded. If not, why would he have used a metaphor of such extreme narrowness as a camel going through the eye of a needle to describe the wealthy entering into Heaven. Even his disciples were perplexed and amazed at His teachings regarding this topic.

Were Jesus' narrow-minded teachings instructing us to become Pharisaical brethren with a mission to cover every jot and tittle (Matthew 5:18)? Or was He, rather, giving us a general description of His *principals* and encouraging us to pick up our cross and follow Him?'

Paul called those at Corinth his "brothers and sisters" (1 Corinthians 1:10) despite their sins documented throughout his letter.

Calling them brethren didn't mean that Paul condoned their sins, and it didn't mean that he accepted their behavior. It meant that, or appeared as though, Paul still *perceived them* as brothers and sisters in Christ.

This was the basis of my frustration. Members of the Lord's church try to follow the examples and commands of our Lord and the first-century church; however, some seem to have a lack of understanding of some of the Scriptures. Their lack of understanding causes others to label, malign, and separate from these brethren instead of reasoning the scriptures together as

God would have us do. Yes, it's easier to label a brother and run… and it is wrong.

Paul called the sinful members of the church of Christ at Corinth "brethren."

So why did Josh believe that he and I were *not* brothers simply because I attended a congregation that supported orphanages? Did I discount *him* as a brother because he attended a congregation that did not do the same?

Our brethren in the corner of emotionalism and ecumenicalism need to come to the center, and our brethren in the corner of caution against emotionalism and the desire for an explicit *Thus saith the Lord* need to come to the center – but what *is* that center? Friend, I do not have the answer at this moment, but it is a question we need to consider.

I am of the firm belief that we cannot sacrifice Truth in an effort toward unity, so this begs the question: is biblical unity even possible in today's fractured body?

It seems to me that achieving complete unity within today's body of Christ is not possible. Perfect unity is possible in theory, as my friend Bradley Cobb has said to me, but it isn't probable because Christian people make up the church, and every Christian struggles with pride, ego, personality traits, differing motives, etc.

Chapter 25
Challenges: Division
A House Divided...

"Grant, we've been away from the Lord and His church for so long. There's so much I need to catch up on," I admitted.

Jonetta and Emily made dinner in their spacious kitchen while Grant and I drank decaf coffee in their living room. Jonetta had brought Lane's mechanical swing – set it up in their kitchen, and he was enjoying the ride. Andrew, Paul, and Noah played with Daniel and Kylee in the den.

"Like what?" asked Grant.

"Like what happened to me at the office a few days ago." I explained the incident with Josh.

"Wow! You knew how to run him off, didn't you?" He laughed. "Michael, you have encountered one of the greatest challenges in the brotherhood today. The challenge of our division."

"I agree. Haven't been able to get it off my mind since it happened," I said.

"Boys," Emily hollered from the kitchen, "dinner will be ready in about 20 minutes!"

I looked at Grant.

"Yeah," he smiled, "she called us *boys*."

"I'm pretty sure that's how our wives see us," I said with a chuckle.

Grant laughed and said, "I should have said, 'Thanks, mom!'"

The laughs passed, and I pressed the issue. "How divided are we?"

"It's hard to say," Grant looked at his cup, "because of the autonomous nature of the Lord's church. But, let's see if we can count out the different divisions in the church."

"Okay." He had my attention.

"There are sets and subsets," Grant appeared to be thinking out loud. "The liberal subset contains those who fellowship everyone religious, some use mechanical instruments, some accept any previous baptism, some have this new 'praise team' thing (I didn't know what that meant, but didn't want to interrupt), some of them disregard the Bible's qualifications of an elder, then there's the whole DMR situation–"

"I'm sorry. DMR?" I interrupted. "Do more resuscitating?"

Grant laughed loudly.

"Good one, Michael!" he said with a laugh. "No, DMR stands for divorce, marriage, and remarriage," he clarified.

"Oh, okay. Got it. Go ahead," I said.

"No, no. Stop me if I lose you. Now, let's see… the liberal subset… some of our brotherhood colleges have become so secular that it's hard to see them as 'brotherhood' schools. The Boston Movement–"

"I read about that a few years ago," I injected.

"Then," Grant continued, "in the conservative subset you have so many that I don't know if I can think of them all. You've got the non-institutional, the one-cuppers–"

"One cuppers?" I interrupted again.

"Yeah – those that use one cup for the fruit of the vine–"

"One cup for *everyone*?" I blurted out.

Grant smiled. "Yeah, one cup for everyone."

"I'd sit in the front pew hoping to be the *first* to get the cup." I was shaking my head.

"Me too, Michael," he laughed. "Okay… one cuppers, those that believe in the use of head coverings, those who don't have separated Bible classes… how many is that?"

I started laughing. "Grant, I lost count!"

"Isn't it sad that there are so many factions that we lose count?" Grant's question was more of a reflective statement, and I could see that it bothered him. It bothered me too.

"You see, Michael, the liberals want to unbind where God binds, and the conservatives want to bind where God doesn't bind," Grant said. "And it's so sad, because if you examine the extreme far end of the liberal side, they believe every religious person is saved, but when you go to the extreme far end of the conservative side, they believe that almost no one is saved except their tiny group that meets together–"

"Just like that Josh guy," I interrupted.

"Exactly!" Grant responded. "He said you weren't his brother in Christ, but he didn't really know anything about you, did he?"

"Nothing more than where we attend church," I replied.

"Exactly," Grant said as he leaned forward in his chair. "And do you think Josh has ever attended any of our services?" he asked.

"I doubt it," I admitted.

"I think you're probably right," Grant responded as he sat his empty coffee cup on a side table. "So why do our brethren feel as though they can make the kind of judgments they make on others in our brotherhood?"

I thought about his question for a moment.

"Boys, sorry to interrupt," Emily came into the room, "but dinner's ready a little early," she said as she rubbed her hands together.

Grant got up, and I followed his lead. He looked at me. "Michael, let's eat!"

Dinner was a lot of fun. Grant and Emily were humble, sincere people. We discussed business, politics, kids, the war in Iraq, parenting, struggles, sins, and the lasagna.

After dinner we gathered up the brood, hugged Grant and Emily, thanked them for everything and loaded up the SUV.

"Grant, how about y'all come to our house next week for dinner and we can finish our talk?" I asked as we stood on their doorstep.

"We'd love to have you both!" Jonetta jumped into the conversation.

"Y'all pick the night and we'll be there," Emily said quickly.

"How about next Thursday?" Jonetta offered. They looked at each and shook their heads.

"Thursday is good for us. What do we bring–"

"I'll give you a call, and we'll work it out, okay?" Jonetta said as she hugged Emily.

"Grant, I ain't hugging you," I said with an ominous look.

"Well, I'm glad, Michael. You're not really my type!" We both laughed and shook hands. If you were looking from a distance, we appeared to be a couple of yuppies. That's funny when you consider how broke Jonetta and I were. I hoped we could scrounge together something to eat for next week's entertainment dinner. Would Grant and Emily like beans and fried bologna?

"You boys better straighten up or I'll have your Dad pull over and I'll spank you both!" We had only been in the Expedition ten minutes and the boys had started arguing.

Jonetta was a drill sergeant when she needed to be, and the boys respected her rank. The fighting in the back seat stopped immediately. Yes, she believed in spanking, and so did I. Call CPS.

Our kids fighting. How do *you*, as a parent, feel when your children bicker and fight? Now ask yourself this… how does God feel when His children bicker and fight? Does our division make God feel this same way?

Chapter 26
Put On Some Socks, Woman!
And Interesting Question about Interpretation

It was the following Thursday evening.

"Michael, look at this." Grant pointed to a verse in my Bible. Grant and Emily were in our home and we were doing our best to be gracious and entertaining hosts.

The kids were wound up. Their laughing and chatter echoed from our open second-story home. Jonetta and Emily worked busily in the kitchen. Lane, perched in his bouncy-cot placed on our kitchen island made baby noises in the middle of the girls' business.

Emily came into our living room. "Y'all have such a beautiful home!" she said to me. If she only knew!

"Thanks, Emily," I responded. "Thank God for Jonetta's decorating abilities!" She agreed and walked back into our kitchen to help Jonetta.

"Jonetta, get Emily some socks – her feet have got to be freezing–"

"No, I'm okay," Emily interrupted from the kitchen. Emily's comment agitated me. Why? Because she had worn a dress and long boots for the evening. She removed her boots when they arrived showing her tan legs and feet with perfectly painted toe-nails.

I wasn't a prude. I was a *man*, and women sometimes forget the incredible power, pull, and temptation they can generate by the exposure of their flesh.

I was trying my absolute best to maintain my restoration to our faith, but was now faced with the lust of the flesh by this innocent sister who was in my home exposing her tan legs and painted toe-nails. John was trying to dig through the dirt. My shameful thoughts… *Satan, get behind me!*

"Michael?" Grant looked at me, realizing that my thoughts were somewhere else.

"Oh, yeah, I'm sorry, Grant. Really sorry – you were saying," my attention snapped back.

"Look at this verse. It was John 17,

> *Neither pray I for these alone, but for them also which shall believe on me through their word; That they all may **be one**; as thou, Father, art in me, and I in thee, that they also may **be one in us**: that the world may believe that thou hast sent me* (John 17: 20-21).

Randall had taught me these verses.

"Michael, Jesus wanted His church to be one. He wanted us all to be in harmony, practicing His faith, His gospel, His instructions in unity and love," Grant explained. "But today's church of Christ is not 'one' in the same mind. Our divided brotherhood is the *proof* that we're not one."

"I don't think that this kind of unity is possible, Grant," I replied.

"Brother, I don't think it is, either. There are simply too many factions," he admitted.

"What," I asked, "would it take for us to obtain this kind of unity?"

Jonetta came into the living room with a small plate of fried cheese sticks. "You guys can eat these while we finish supper," she said.

"Awesome!" Grant grabbed one from the plate. I, on the other hand, was mentally stressing about how we were going pay our electric bill that was now two weeks past due.

"Thank you, Jonetta," I said, pulling her into a quick hug. I was so proud of her, and thankful that she was not showing off *her* legs and feet!

Grant chewed on the hot cheese stick and considered my question. "Well, for our brotherhood to obtain the unity that Christ desires would mean that everyone in the church would need to reconsider *how* they interpret the Bible."

"I'm not following," I admitted.

"I have a good friend named Dennis, and he's brought up some excellent questions that every Christian should think about. Primarily, how do we interpret the Scriptures?"

"Go on," I encouraged Grant with sincere interest.

"For example, Michael, why do some congregations insist on using one cup in the Lord's Supper, while others use multiple cups? It's all in how they interpret the Bible.

In other words, you have two sincere, honest-hearted Christians who perceive the Bible's instructions a little differently, right?"

"Right," I agreed.

"So you've got two good-hearted, God-fearing people who have been baptized into Christ and who are sincerely *trying their best* to do what God wants them to do, right?"

"Yeah," I followed.

"So why does Christian A believe that one cup is what God wants, but Christian B believes that multiple cups are what God wants?" Grant put forth the question.

I sat back and mulled his question. "Grant, each side can make a strong case–"

"That is exactly right, Michael! Each side can argue the case successfully. Each side can justify their positions with scripture, with scriptural principles, and with passion. So which one is biblically correct?"

"Well, it is in their interpretation–"

"Brother," Grant exclaimed, "you've identified the problem that most of our brethren won't deal with!

"It is our interpretation," he continued, "that is at the heart of our division. Look, Michael, the big things are easy to interpret: One body, the church (Colossians 1:18; Ephesians 4:4). One baptism in water (Acts 2:38; Galatians 3:26-27; Ephesians 4:4; 1 Peter 3:21). Taking the Lord's Supper on the first day of the week (Acts 20:7). Singing, using the one, perfect, mechanical instrument from God – our vocal cords (Ephesians 5:19). These commands of God are easy to identify. No deep interpretation is needed.

"It's when we begin to draw lines in the sand over issues that are more ambiguous, like–"

"Like using one cup," I interrupted.

"Exactly," Grant said. "Michael, I've heard it said, and I don't remember where, but the saying is this, 'We should have unity in essentials, liberty in non-essentials, and in all things, charity.'"

His logic and rationale was difficult to argue and the phrase struck a chord in my heart. I didn't seek to be a progressive liberal, nor did I seek to be a rule-keeping Pharisee.

I wanted to be nothing more than a New Testament Christian – a man after God's own heart. Was that possible?

According to the liberals, I was a Pharisee. According to the Pharisees, I was a liberal.

What was I according to God?

Chapter 27

A Preacher in Danger

March 2005: Lake Dallas, Texas

March, 2005:

The boys were exhausted, and so were we. The entire Saturday had been spent packing the U-Haul. I had backed the truck up close to the garage door, and it was getting dark.

Jonetta did a final check of the house – nothing was left. The plans were to get a hotel room in Denton, TX, and leave early the following morning toward Illinois.

We said our good-byes to the dozens of brethren who had come to help us pack. Their love was incredible. Many brought food, two ladies took care of the baby while Jonetta worked, and the rest had worked tirelessly throughout the day.

The entire group gathered in our driveway at the end of the day, and we prayed together. It was an uplifting experience that we would never forget.

Everyone had left our home and I was pulling the door down on the U-Haul when I heard his voice.

"Are you Michael Shank?"

A heavy-set man wearing khaki pants and a white button-down shirt appeared at the back corner of the moving truck a couple of feet from the garage door opening. We shook hands.

"I'm Michael, and you are…?"

"My name is Adam Thurst. I am the minister of the church of Christ–"

"You're the minister of the congregation we visited last fall," I interrupted.

"Well, yes. I think you visited with us–"

"In August and September," I finished his sentence. It had been seven months since we had visited this particular congregation… robots and the old lady.

"And it's taken you this long to follow up with us?" I said as I turned back to latch the U-Haul door.

"Well, uh, I guess it's been a while."

"Look," I stepped close to the sorry excuse of a preacher. "My family and I have been through Hell because of my sins and selfishness." I didn't realize that I was in his face, walking forward as he stepped backward toward his car.

"We were trying to come back to the Lord when we visited your congregation and it's taken you seven months to even realize that we were there?"

I also had not been aware of the inward hostility and bitterness I harbored toward this congregation, and this man was about to receive the brunt of my anger. He

back-peddled as I walked forward, staying in his face.
We had almost reached his car which he had parked at the
curb of our front yard.

"And you show up on the day that we're moving out
of here? Half a year later? Are you kidding me?" I was
yelling.

Adam, completely pale-faced, fumbled for his car
keys. I, unfortunately, had lost my temper and was ready
to give the guy a good beating. "John" was still there
trying his best to dominate me, and John was winning at
that moment.

"Adam, if you know what's good for you, you'll get
in that car and get out of here right now—"

"Michael!" Jonetta shouted from the garage. Adam
tripped a little as he opened his car door. After managing
to get into this car, he started the engine, looked at me
with a crazed look, and sped away.

"Michael, what is wrong with you?" she shouted. I
really didn't care. Adam's visit this long after we'd
visited his congregation was bad form. I hoped my
reaction might motivate him to re-think his approach at
follow-ups with visitors to their congregation.

"Honey, don't worry about it. I was just having a little discussion with... a hireling." My attitude and behavior was sinful; however, sometimes people need a jolt.

Preachers preach because they have a burning desire to proclaim the gospel. Others, in my opinion, preach because it is a "job."

Is the latter of the two a hireling? Just asking.

Chapter 28

Here is *Real* Hope

March 2006: Carterville, Illinois

March, 2006: One Year Later.

Life was actually good again. We were spiritually stronger than we had ever been. Personal reflection of my sins, in combination of God's forgiveness and grace, caused me to cling to Him as never before.

It had taken countless hours of prayers, and (I think) there were actually calluses on my knees! I had spent a lot of days during the past year fasting and weeping over my past sins. The bitter tears that flowed from my eyes over the things that I had done to the Lord, my family, and the church would have filled a five-gallon bucket.

Jonetta and I, with thanks be to God, had become an active and integral part of the church of Christ close to our new home in Carterville, Illinois (a modest rental home located at the corner of Greenbriar Road and Country Club Lane). We were doing our dead-level best to produce the fruits of repentance (Luke 3:8).

Repentance is the hard part. Anyone can say, "I love God." Many will profess their belief in Jesus Christ when asked, but repentance? That's where the rubber meets the road. Giving up your own will and self-desire might be one of the most challenging things a man or woman can do to themselves.

Jonetta and I weren't perfect – not even close, and we didn't pretend to be. We just wanted to live our lives in His service. And for the first time in my life, humility defined my personality.

We took great hope in Paul's words,

> *In whom we have redemption through his blood, the forgiveness of sins, according to the riches of his grace; wherein he hath abounded toward us in all wisdom and prudence* (Ephesians 1:7-8).

It is a remarkable and unfathomable thing to consider that the One, Supreme, Sovereign Creator of all things can and will forgive our most heinous behavior when we, Christians who have sinned, make the decision to trust His grace and His promises.

It was just as Jonetta had said when she was trying to convince me that there was still hope,

> *And these things write we unto you, that your joy may be full. This then is the message which we have heard of him, and declare unto you, that God is light, and in him is no darkness at all. If we say that we have fellowship with him, and walk in*

darkness, we lie, and do not the truth: But
if we walk in the light, as he is in the light,
we have fellowship one with another, and
the blood of Jesus Christ his Son cleanseth
us from all sin. If we say that we have no
sin, we deceive ourselves, and the truth is
not in us. If we confess our sins, he is
faithful and just to forgive us our sins, and
to cleanse us from all unrighteousness. If
we say that we have not sinned, we make
him a liar, and his word is not in us (1
John 1:4-10).

John wrote these things by the direction of God's
Spirit and they were written that we might be full!
Fullness begins with owning our sins, admitting that we
do sin, and confessing our sins. It is this humble attitude
that brings us to God's throne and demonstrates our
willingness to *trust* Him.

This trust, combined with our desire to obey God,
defines true faith. Trust and obey, for there's no other
way to be happy in Jesus, but to trust and obey. Aren't
these the words we sing in exhorting, teaching, and
admonishing one another?

Trust and obedience is faith manifested in the flesh. "Faith" (our trust in the Lord and our obedience to His Word) *allows* God the opportunity to cleanse us from *all* sin and unrighteousness.

Brother and sister, hope can again be yours! God wants you to again be filled with that hope found in Christ Jesus and in His abundant forgiveness.

Brother and sister, you have hope! Consider Jeremiah 29:11-13,

> *For I know the thoughts that I think toward you, saith the LORD, thoughts of peace, and not of evil, to give you an expected end. Then shall ye call upon me, and ye shall go and pray unto me, and I will hearken unto you. And ye shall seek me, and find me, when ye shall search for me with all your heart.*

What does God *think* toward you? In His unfathomable love He thinks thoughts of peace, not evil. He desires your willingness to call upon Him and to pray to Him. When you finally bring your broken self before Him and seek him with all of your heart, you will find Him again!

But there is a great obstacle before each one of us who has left the Lord: our memory. Our memory stands as a torturer. When we remember our sins, we relive the pain that we have caused others.

Our memory ushers in the guilt and shame associated with those sins. This leads us to an erroneous thought: *God cannot and will not forgive me.* Shame has killed many good men.

Hope conquers the shame and guilt associated with the *memory* of our past sins. If I could write one thing on the template of a tortured man's heart, it would be this,

> *For I will be merciful to their unrighteousness, and their sins and their iniquities **will I remember no more*** (Hebrews 8:12).

Friend, God has an ability that you and I do not possess, nor can we truly ever understand; He has the exclusive ability to put our sins in a place where He never remembers them again. Now *that* is real hope!

Chapter 29
Amish Aren't the Only Ones Who Shun
April 2006: Carterville, Illinois

April, 2006: Carterville, Illinois

A friend of mine had given me the opportunity to partner with him in his electrical contracting company. The new field interested me and the opportunity to franchise his operation appealed to my experiences in starting, operating, and selling businesses.

He trained and licensed me through an apprenticeship and the business grew rapidly.

The congregation we had attended for the past year was close to our Carterville home, and it was one of the larger congregations in our area. Most southern Illinois congregations consisted of ten to sixty members, but our congregation had 150 members – a "mega-church" among the churches of Christ in our area.

Jonetta and I attended every service and function. While she helped with classes, women's Bible study groups, and the young children's group, I served at the Lord's Table, led prayer, and had been given the opportunity to do short devotionals at the end of our Wednesday night Bible study service. I was, as they say, on fire again.

The latter part of Luke 12:48 drove me,

For unto whomsoever much is given, of him shall be much required: and to whom men have committed much, of him they will ask the more. God's forgiveness of my wretchedness was a motivator of love and service in return.

One Sunday evening after services Jonetta and I were finishing a piece of cheesecake at Ryan's Restaurant in Marion, Illinois.

"Honey, that's Jack and Donna Rendleman," I said looking to the other side of the large restaurant.

"Hey, it is!" she replied. They were old friends and brethren from another congregation.

"I'm gonna go over and say hello," I said while wiping my mouth. The crowd was packed around the end of the buffet where a man in a chef hat cut prime rib for the all-you-can-eat buffet folks.

"Excuse me. Excuse me." I said politely, trying to get around a big guy who thought I was going to take his piece of prime-rib. He grunted and didn't move. I diverted another direction and came around his left flank, stepping by him.

As I moved toward Jack and Donna's table, Donna saw me and whispered something to Jack. He turned quickly toward me.

"Jack?" I greeted him with an extended hand.

"Heard you were back in this area," Jack said as he looked across at Donna, not extending a hand in return.

"You still married?"

"Yeah, uh… of course. Jonetta and I have four boys now." I replied with a growing realization that my old friends, brothers and sisters in Christ, were "shunning" me.

"That's a surprise… surprise that you're *still* married," he and Donna laughed at what seemed to be an "inside" joke.

"Figured that a playboy like you would be on your third or fourth wife by now," Jack spit it out like a threat as he turned toward me, finally looking me in the eye.

Adrenaline pumped through my veins as shame enveloped my mind and heart. It was as if someone had stripped me naked for the world to see. My sins had been the substance of brotherhood gossip and it was a shock to my system.

People that I loved, respected, and considered to be friends had turned against me. I didn't blame Jack.

"Very sorry, Jack. Just thought I'd say hello. Donna, my best to you and the children." What else was there to say? He was right.

.

"Were they happy to see you?" Jonetta asked.

I smiled and sat back down at our table. "I don't think *happy* is the right word," I said while picking up a fork.

"What's wrong?" she was concerned.

"Well," I poked the fork into the graham cracker crust of what remained of the cheesecake at the edge of the plate.

"Let's just say…" a tear rolled down my cheek, "that an old friendship is ruined"

"Michael, what happened?" Momma was going into protection mode.

"Honey," I laid down the fork. "This is a small community–"

"So–" she interrupted.

"So, it seems as though Jack and Donna are pretty disappointed in me," I admitted.

"Michael, what'd they say?"

I replayed the event to her. When you live in a small town, everyone knows what you do. Jack and Donna had heard the gossip years before. They'd heard about my drinking, infidelity, and unfaithfulness to the church. Now they were simply showing their disdain. It was their golden opportunity to make their feelings known.

Good for them. I deserved it all.

"I'm going over there—" Jonetta started to jump up from the table, but I grabbed her hand.

"Jonetta, please sit down—"

"Michael, if you think for a minute that I'm going to put up with that kind of self-righteous piety—"

"Jonetta, *please* sit down," I begged. Women have the power to let a man *be* a man, or they won't.

Her eyes were lit up with anger, but she slowly sat down.

"Look. I've come to terms with it, but I hadn't thought about those that I had negatively affected by my sins. Jack and Donna... honey, it's my fault. Don't blame them. They're just reacting to what they've heard," I said while picking at the cheesecake.

"But Michael, you got Jack his job at [a well-known investment firm]. And how long ago was that? Nine years? And their family? How many hundreds of dollars of groceries did I buy for Donna and deliver to their home when they were struggling–"

"Jonetta, it doesn't matter now," I said.

"Well it *should* matter. They've got a lot of nerve thinking that they're so righteous that they can treat you that way–"

"Hey," I interrupted.

"What?" she blurted out. She was seething with anger.

"How about we rent a movie?"

Jonetta's look said, "*I know you're just trying to change the subject, but I'll go along with it for your sake.*"

"Umm, what do you want to get?" she asked.

"How about… Brokeback Mountain?" I smiled. She literally lost it. I hadn't seen her laugh that hard in a long time.

I waited until she composed herself as I did my best to seem serious.

"Yeah," she looked at me with those big blue eyes and asked, "Brokeback Mountain? Like *you* really want to see a movie about *homosexuals*?"

I started laughing. "It's a gay movie? Really?" I feigned surprise. "Well, in that case–"

"Let's get War of the Worlds," she suggested.

"Excellent! I like Tom Cruise, but not in a gay way!" I said as we stood up from our table.

She laughed and said, "So glad you clarified that, honey!"

I left a tip and took Jonetta by the hand. We looked over toward Jack and Donna's table as we walked out. They quickly looked away, raising their posture as if to say, "We are *so* much better than you."

We got into the Ford Expedition and I started the engine.

"Jonetta, I'm sorry," I said as I looked at her sitting in the passenger seat.

"Sorry for what, Michael?" She asked with the kindest face.

"I'm sorry for ruining our family name," I said.

"Husband," she said as she looked at me with intensity, "if they don't have it in their heart to forgive, that's not *your* fault. And if they can't forgive *you*, then they're gonna have a big problem on the Day of Judgment [2 Corinthians 5:10]."

I pulled out of the parking lot and thought of Matthew 6,

> *For if ye forgive men their trespasses, your heavenly Father will also forgive you: But if ye forgive not men their trespasses, neither will your Father forgive your trespasses* (vv. 14-15).

I just wished that my brothers and sisters would forgive me.

Chapter 30
Comfort Zones
June 2006: Carterville, Illinois

June, 2006:

"Michael, you need to do this!" Nick was emphatic.

"I'm not comfortable," I replied

"You don't have to be comfortable. Just take advantage of this opportunity to serve the Lord!" he continued.

"So, they need someone to fill in for them two times each month?" I asked

"Yeah, you'd preach for them on the first and third Sundays every month," Nick replied. "And doesn't pay much, but–"

"Nick, I don't care if they pay me a dime. It's not about the money," I said.

"Okay, how about I call them and get you set up for the first and third Sundays with the first month being a trial-type agreement?"

I agreed. Preaching the gospel excited me and the money didn't matter. I simply wanted to be useful to God, and if they paid enough to cover my gas then that was a bonus!

I still doubted that God wanted *me* to preach, but if He was willing to open a door, then I would try my best to step through to the opportunity.

Nick made the arrangements.

It was the first Sunday of the following month. I parked our SUV at the rear of the little church building in DuQuoin, Illinois. A few brethren were filing into the building. I looked at my Bible.

"Dear Father, please help me to proclaim your Word in Truth, in Spirit, and with passion. Father, help me not to make any mistakes with your Word and may all the things that we do this morning be pleasing in your sight. In Jesus' name, Amen."

After going inside and greeting all ten of the brethren, it was easy to see that they were excited that I was there. This small, fledgling congregation of Christians had met together at this building for over forty years.

We prayed and sang with fervor and passion, and then it was time for me to preach my first sermon.

After services concluded, brethren hugged and kissed me, and thanked me for driving so far from Carterville to help them. It was actually *my* honor.

These brethren had invited me to preach to them. They had invested their trust into my feeble abilities.

This was the beginning. Over the next two years I would hone my skills, trying to memorize every sermon. I had secretly loathed preachers who read from a script, and that loathing motivated me to make a decision: try to memorize the lesson or don't preach the lesson. Just *never* read from a script!

My son would say, "Daddy, get up there, draw back, and let it fly!" He was talking about the way he wanted me to preach.

Every sermon *could* be compelling. Every sermon *could* be delivered with the fervor and excitement of Marshall Keeble. That was the goal.

How do we grow? We're put in situations out of our comfort zone. When we are moved to the outside of our comfort zone, we have two options: quit or rise to the occasion.

In my mind, I wasn't a preacher. I wasn't worthy to stand in the pulpit. I wasn't worthy to accept a dime for any efforts that I had put forth. I certainly wasn't worthy of any good that came from these efforts. No man is worthy – and I was the *most* unworthy of all men.

However, the Lord had a plan for a broken, weak, and humiliated man.

Chapter 31
Wanna Be a Preacher's Wife?
August 2008: Carterville, Illinois

August, 2008: Carterville, Illinois

Two years had passed since my first sermon at DuQuoin, Illinois, and part-time preaching had become a passion. There was no other way to put it. I didn't care if I ever made a penny from preaching. The gospel had to be preached. It had to be done by men who understood the power of the gospel and the power of God's love and forgiveness.

I was content working my electrical business during the day and preaching on a "fill-in" basis on Sundays. Paul made tents and preached the gospel. I was thrilled to be doing the same.

I had just finished preaching at the little church in DuQuoin one Lord's Day in August. A young couple in their 30's was visiting that morning. I walked over to greet them.

"It's so good to have y'all here this morning," I said with a hug and handshake.

"It's always good to be here. We come up about every year," said the young woman. My name is Teresa, and this is my husband, Don."

She introduced their children and I shook the kid's hands. What a great Christian family. The kids were a little quiet as kids are in new settings, but this couple seemed to have a spark in their eyes.

"Mike," she continued, "we are looking for a preacher at Metropolis. You really need to come down and try out–"

"Oh, Teresa," I interrupted, "thanks so much, but I'm not really looking to preach full-time."

"Why not? You are really good and you have such energy–"

"Thanks so much, but... I work in the electric business and we're pretty happy in Carterville–"

"Mike, you should come down and visit. Why not try out?" She wasn't pushy, just very sincere. Don and Teresa were good people. They were the kind of people you'd invite to dinner in your home or want to hang out with at a ball game.

"Well," I said with reservation, "I'll think about it."

"Could I get your phone number? I'll have one of our elders call." She pulled out a piece of paper and an ink pen. Teresa wrote down my number. We gathered up our things and said our goodbyes.

"Dear Father, You *don't* want me to preach full-time, do you?" The hot August sun beat down through the windshield as I made my way back to Carterville.

"Lord, you've blessed us so much and we want to serve you, but you surely don't want us to go to Metropolis, do You?"

The field corn was a tall blur out of the right-side passenger window as I sped south down Highway 149. The town of Hurst, Illinois, was just ahead.

"Lord, I don't want to be a full-time preacher, and I know *you* don't want me to be a full-time preacher," the prayer continued.

An Illinois state trooper was parked just outside of Hurst. "Whoa, slow down, slow down!" I said out loud. The female trooper was looking down at something in her car. Lucky break.

"I'm sorry, Lord." Prayers get interrupted when you're driving. "Forgive me for speeding, and forgive me for assuming to know your will. I will go wherever you lead. I just hope you don't lead us to Metropolis."

Jonetta and the kids were at the house 45 minutes before I arrived. The boys were playing in the backyard and she was grilling hamburgers.

"Honey, a couple asked me to try out for a full-time preaching position down at Metropolis," I said as she flipped a burger.

"You're kidding?" she turned to me in surprise.

"No kidding," I said, looking at the flames in the grill. *"Hellfire would be awful,"* I thought to myself

"Well, are you going to do it?" She asked.

"Don't really want to," I admitted.

"Why?"

"Well," I picked up her glass of iced tea, "I'm not sure that I'm ready for that kind of responsibility. Besides, we're happy here. Things are going well–"

"Michael," she grabbed her iced tea out of my hand, "first, get your own iced tea. Second," she flipped another burger, "you'd better be asking what God wants instead of what *you* want."

"Do *you* want to be a *preacher's wife?*" I raised my voice in surprise.

"No, I don't! But it doesn't matter what I want. If that's what God wants, I'll be happy," she said with an effort to calm my emotions.

"Seriously?" I was shocked.

"Yes, honey. If that's what God wants you to do, I'll support you," she said as she turned off the grill. "Boys, come in and get washed up!"

Eight hours later:

We arrived home after the evening worship services. The boys wanted to play a little more in the backyard. It was August and the sky didn't get fully dark until around 8:45pm.

Jonetta was cutting watermelon slices for the kids and I prepared the new week's job quotes at the computer.

The phone rang and Jonetta answered it.

"Yes, he's right here," she said and handed me the phone.

"Hello?"

"Mike, this is Edgar, I'm one of the elders down here at Metropolis," his voice was older, but very upbeat. "You met Teresa and her family this morning," he said.

"Oh, yeah, hello," I was surprised that he had called so soon.

"She said you might be a pretty good preacher, but I don't think much of her opinion," he said with a laugh. He had a sense of humor.

"Well, uh, thanks–"

"This is the best congregation in a five state area. We need to talk…"

Chapter 32
But Jonah Rose
Up To Flee

September 2008: Carterville, Illinois

Two Sundays later I was in the Metropolis pulpit, preaching my heart out! I didn't want the job, as strange as that sounds.

So why was I there? I feared the possibility that *not* going would have been rejecting a path that God wanted me to follow.

The congregation was small, but the people were wonderful. They had asked me to teach and preach for the entire day, but I had a previous commitment at our home congregation and could only preach morning service. Preaching as an "applicant" was more of an audition than an interview.

Talking with the brethren after the service was enjoyable. They were sincere and down to earth. Edgar then drove us to the parsonage. We usually don't refer to the preacher's home as a parsonage, but it's easier to say parsonage than it is to say "the house that the congregation provides to the preacher and his family." It was a nice brick ranch with a fenced in back yard.

"Daddy, is this our new house?" Noah beamed with excitement.

"No, no, son. We're just looking at it," I replied.

"Why?" he asked with confusion.

"Well, because it *might* be our house someday," I replied.

"When?" Noah asked.

"Son, ask your momma." Sometimes dads pass the buck when they're stuck.

Four nights later:

The phone in the kitchen rang.

"Hello?" I answered the phone.

"Is this the electrified preacher?" he asked.

I laughed. It was Edgar. "Yeah, and this sounds like Edgar?"

"Yeah. Hey, the church really likes you and your preaching. But you didn't give us a full day, and a lot of them said they thought you were just trying to promote your new video," he said.

I had discussed my DVD during my previous sermon at Metropolis. It was a video that I had completed in cooperation with the World Video Bible School in Maxwell, Texas, entitled, "Why Are There So Many Churches?"

"I'm sorry they felt that way. That wasn't my intention–"

"Why don't you come back down and do a full day with us?" he interrupted. "It'll give everyone a chance to see what you're made of." Edgar was a man used to getting his way.

"When are you thinking?" I asked.

"How about this coming Sunday?" He asked.

"Uh." I was scrambling for our calendar. "Edgar, I can't make it this Sunday, but maybe the next Sunday–"

"That'll be fine," he interrupted. "You bring your family and be here about 9:30. We'll start our class at 10:00. You'll teach the adult Bible class and preach morning and evening."

"Okay, uh… we'll be there," I responded reluctantly. Edgar hung up the phone.

"Michael, what'd he say?" Jonetta said to my back.

I spun around. "They want us to come back!" I responded as if I had just been struck by lightning.

"That's wonderful!" she exclaimed. "When?"

"It's *not* wonderful," I responded with bitterness.

"Why would you say that, Michael?" Jonetta said as she drew closer to me.

"Because we both know that I am not worthy to do this work," I admitted while looking at the tiled kitchen floor.

"Sweetheart," she said as she put her arms around my waist. "No one is worthy enough."

"But why *me*?" I begged. "It makes no sense. Edgar said they have already tried-out twelve men. Men with degrees in Theology, and experience–"

"Michael, your preaching is different… you don't do the standard kind of sermon. Your preaching is…"

"Weird?" I offered with a smile.

"Yeah," she smiled. "It's definitely weird!"

"'Seriously, Jonetta, I can't understand this." My anxiety was peaking. "I told God that I was concerned. I told Him that I did not want to be a full-time preacher–"

"Well, that's probably it," she interrupted.

"What's it?" I asked.

"That's probably *why* God is opening this door. Michael, you don't *want* the title, the money, or anything else that goes along with being a 'preacher.' Your motivation is to follow God's guidance and try to do what is right."

Did I say she was a wise woman?

"So when are we going back?" Jonetta asked.

"Not this Sunday, but the Sunday after," I replied. My face evidently said something more.

"Michael, what's wrong?"

"It's just...well...I just know that God doesn't really want *me* to preach full time," I responded while looking into her eyes.

"Michael, you do *not* know that–"

"Well, I tell you what I'm going to do," I said as I broke free from her hug and opened the refrigerator door.

"I'll make *sure* they won't hire me."

"How are you going to do that?" Jonetta questioned.

"I'm gonna tell 'em the truth... that I have no degree in Theology, that I have hardly any experience in preaching, and that I feel completely unworthy to stand in the pulpit. What choice will they have? They will be forced to hire one of the other guys."

Chapter 33
The Foolishness of God
Is Wiser Than Men
September 2008: Carterville, Illinois

September, 2008:

I sat in the small church office at Metropolis, looking across the room at Edgar and Stan – the two elders of the congregation. Edgar sat in the leather chair behind the desk. This was the final interview and Edgar seemed to be the "ruling" elder of the two.

"So what do you think of our congregation?" asked Edgar. It had been a couple of weeks since I had done the "entire day" of teaching and preaching.

And my "strategy" had not worked. What was my premeditated strategy that was supposed to ensure that the congregation would not want to hire me, along with making sure that God would not want me to preach? It was simple: stand in the pulpit, admit that I was unworthy to be there, confess that their other candidates were much better choices than I was because I had no Bible degree, and be as humble as possible. I called it a *strategy*, but it was all entirely true.

The problem? It had not worked. Why did they want *me*?

"I think this is a congregation of great Christian people," I admitted. "The house is beautiful and I have no objections to anything," I said to the two elders.

"Now, as far as your weekly pay–"

"Brother," I interrupted Edgar. "It doesn't matter and I'd rather not talk about it," I said firmly.

Edgar and Stan looked at each other with confusion.

"Look," I continued, "my feeling is this… if God really wants us here, He'll take care of our needs, and so the pay really doesn't matter, does it?"

"When can you start?" Stan asked with a laugh. He was a well-groomed, up-beat guy.

"I'd have to give my partner a six week notice," I responded.

"So, that'd put us about the end of October," Edgar stated.

"I think so," I was looking at the calendar on my Blackberry. "We could move on Friday, October 31st, and I could preach the following Sunday, November 2nd. Is that okay with y'all?"

"That sounds like a good plan," Edgar said. Both men stood up and I followed their lead. We all expressed our excitement, gratitude, and a hope for the future of the congregation at Metropolis.

They had interviewed/auditioned thirteen men in total. All of them had some type of Bible degree, except

me. Several were fresh out of a Bible College. Most had
many years of experience, except me. Most were, from
what I had heard, good speakers. Most all of them were
very "qualified." And all of them had been calling Edgar
to inquire if they were going to be hired.

I, the most unqualified of the pool, and evidently the
only man who did not really want to be a full-time
preacher, was hired.

I wasn't proud. I didn't feel like I had won a
victory. I was confused. Completely confused.

Their reason for hiring me boiled down to two
things: humility and an excitement for the gospel.

I drove north on Highway 45 toward Vienna,
Illinois. A doe jumped across my path and I almost got
her. The deer were beginning to move. Shotgun season
was approaching.

A preacher. I mulled the words over in my mind.
Could I live up to their expectations? Fear dominated my
thoughts. *Was I ready? Was I worthy?* No. I wasn't
ready or worthy. But, evidently someone far more
important than those elders, or myself, thought I was
ready.

"Father, I beg you, please help me to help these brethren. I am flawed, and weak, and I commit sin as you know." Tears began to form. "But I can't let the church down. I can't let *you* down. Lord, the only thing I have to offer You is this, I will do my very best for You and this great Cause of Jesus Christ," I prayed out loud as the tears, the ones that had previously been trying to grow, finally flowed down my cheeks.

Then I began to laugh. Have you ever laughed and cried at the same time? What a weird feeling! What a big baby! I cried out of sheer awe of where we had been in life, and simultaneously laughed over the excitement and fear of where God was now leading us. It was the most bizarre place in the history of my life. I was a happy, forgiven, flawed Christian man who had a good business and a life that our entire family enjoyed; yet, I was now going to be a full-time preacher… a position that I didn't want, even to the point of thinking that a strategy of blatant, self-destructive honesty would cause them to throw me out of the building.

"Lord," I prayed again. "I still think you've got the wrong guy, and I'd bet a lot of brethren would agree with me. But I'll do the best I can for You. In Jesus' name I pray. Amen."

Paul's words came to my mind,

> *Now unto him that is able to do exceeding abundantly above all that we ask or think, according to the power that worketh in us* (Ephesians 3:20).

Brother and sister, if you are feeling like there's no hope, God said He is able to do exceeding abundantly above all that we ask or *think*!

Brother and sister, God has a plan for *you.* This statement begs the question, "How do you get out of the mire and vomit that you are in at *this* moment so that you can move toward a life of forgiveness, peace, hope, and service to the Cause of Jesus Christ?"

Chapter 34
Moving Into the Parsonage
October 31st, 2008: Metropolis, Illinois

"Hey, watch it, watch it!" I exclaimed as the dog ran in circles around my legs, wrapping his leash around my knees.

"Gauge," I scolded, "stop!" I shouted before hitting the ground.

The boys were standing at the edge of our open garage door, laughing uncontrollably as they watched me fall over the dog.

"Oh, you stupid dog!" I muttered.

Jonetta, also laughing almost hysterically, walked across the yard to help me get untied. Gauge, our large chocolate lab, stood over me. After tumbling on top of him, he quickly moved over me, trying desperately to lick my face while I struggled on the ground to get free of the leash around my legs. Hog-tied!

It was Halloween. We had almost finished unloading our belongings from the U-Haul into the parsonage. The little Metropolis subdivision teemed with children dressed as ghosts, witches, and creepy things. Adults followed close behind – all of them now watching the new "idiot" of the neighborhood.

"That's the funniest thing!" She laughed out the words as she walked toward me.

"I'm good – it's all good!" I announced as I jumped up from the grass. She laughed harder.

"What a way to start out," I whispered into her ear as she hugged me. Gauge, now in fear for his life, sat by my feet with the leash still attached. The passing crowd of costumed children and parents laughed at my fall over the dog, then moved on with their Trick or Treating.

"Well, you've given the neighbors a good show!" She whispered back into my ear. "At least you didn't accidently curse at the dog," she said through continued laughter. Her giggle box had been turned over.

"That would have been awful!" I admitted. "Can you imagine what people would be saying right now? Hey, did you hear that new preacher cuss at that dog?" We both laughed as we hugged each other.

A few boxes remained in the U-Haul. They were in the front of the truck in that overhead area they call *Mom's Attic*. It was funny because the boxes we had put up there were all marked "Attic."

I walked gingerly down the aluminum ramp that extended out of the back of the big truck and into the open garage, then tripped at the bottom of the ramp causing two boxes in my arms to topple off, hitting the garage floor.

The two boxes burst open. Files, papers, and books slid across the concrete. As we gathered up the mess, there was an old spiral bound notebook that had been hidden away for 20 years. On the cover was scribbled,

Conversion Story: 1988

It was the story of our conversion that I had written twenty years before. The notebook had been put into a *keepsake* box and forgotten until *that* day.

You see, I had documented the entire account of our studies with Randall, in detail, and just as the story had happened. It was all recorded during and following the days of our baptism into Christ.

Why did I document the story as it happened? It began as an effort to refute Randall's biblical arguments, but I continued to write the story as it evolved because of my love of writing.

I had also wanted an accurate record of our study together, because I thought that it would be useful in the future if I ever encountered someone else from the church of Christ!

After our obedience to the gospel, I threw the story in a box, never considering the idea of sharing it with anyone.

Why wouldn't I want to share this story? First, I didn't want anyone to know what kind of person I was prior to my conversion. Second, it seemed like a *testimonial*, and members of the Lord's church did *not* do testimonials.

"Michael, what is that?" asked Jonetta, now trying to see the pages that I quickly flipped through.

"Wow, I'd forgotten about this–"

"What is it?" she demanded.

I closed the book to show her the cover.

"You're kidding," Jonetta responded in shock. "Is that our story from when we were baptized?"

"It is," I grinned.

"Sweetheart," she grabbed my arm. "That would be a book that would help so many–"

"No way," I quickly interrupted.

"Why?" she was genuinely surprised at my response.

"Jonetta, there's no way that I'd ever want anyone knowing what kind of person I was before we were baptized—"

"Michael, you can't worry about that," she countered.

"No, absolutely not! Besides, it's just a long testimonial, and we don't do testimonials in the church of Christ." I was adamant.

Jonetta would spend the next three years trying to convince me to send the story to a publisher.

Chapter 35
What Are You Going To Call It?
April 2011: Metropolis, Illinois

April 2011:

I sat at our dining room table, watching the hummingbirds just outside the east window and sipping on a cup of strong black coffee.

God *had* done exceeding abundantly above everything that we had asked for or thought possible (Ephesians 3:20).

I had just got off the phone and sat back down at the table to think. One of our two elders had called to pass along an encouraging message.

"Preacher-man," the elder said from his end of the phone, "the church has never been happier, and the brethren are saying that we've never had a better preacher."

"Brother, thanks so much for sharing this with me. I don't know what to say–"

"Just keep it up! And don't get a big head," he said with a laugh. "Talk to you later." The phone went dead. It was his customary ending to every phone call.

We were in our third year of service to the church at Metropolis. As I watched the hummingbirds, I reflected on all that the Lord had done in our short time with them.

God had blessed the work beyond our wildest imaginations. The church was excited and growing. It was unbelievable that God had been able to use such a flawed man as me – a man who hadn't even wanted the job to begin with, and a man who, at one point, didn't believe he could ever be forgiven – much less "useful!"

We had grown from 55 to 98. 32 baptisms, 4 restorations, and the church was vibrant with enthusiasm.

*And none of it had to do with me – it was all by, for, and through Jesus Christ. No flesh should ever glory in God's presence (1 Corinthians 1:29), and no pot could take the Potter's credit. God received all of the honor, glory, credit and praise. Yes, God **must** receive all of the glory!*

Jonetta, still in her pajamas, walked over to the coffeepot. She poured herself a cup of coffee, then squirted four pumps of French vanilla creamer into her cup while eye-balling the old spiral bound notebook on the dining room table… our conversion story.

She had finally convinced me to send the story to a few publishers. It had taken her three years to convince me that it was the right thing to do. Thank God for a good woman. Thank God for a good woman!

"Michael, what are you going to call it?" she asked with a smile as she stirred her coffee.

"I'm going to call it… *Muscle and a Shovel.*"

Chapter 36

Cancer in the body of Jesus Christ

February 2015

How did I come back to the Lord Jesus Christ? Brother and sister, if you have been away from the Lord for *any* reason, God deeply desires you to return to Him.

There is a set of very succinct, easy-to-follow, biblical steps that will open a wonderful path for you if you are ready to come back to the Lord. These steps will not only bring you *back* to Jesus Christ, they will keep you from ever falling and failing again!

However, I ask you to forgive me for the need to speak *first* to our faithful brothers and sisters in Christ. If you wish to get right to these steps, go directly to Chapter 38.

To you who are faithful: thank you for your love, patience, forgiveness, support, and understanding. Your love and encouragement has been a fuel that keeps us moving forward in the great Cause of Christ.

While we loved our time in full-time ministry and cherish the relationships Jonetta and I developed during our service to the congregation at Metropolis, I have come to realize that the Lord was leading us toward something further. That *something* was *Muscle and a Shovel*.

You see, if I had *not* been hired by the church to preach in a full time capacity, we would have never moved into the church's parsonage. And if we would have never moved into the parsonage, I would have never dropped that box that contained our old conversion story. That box would have remained in our attic, untouched for who knows how long.

Upon dropping that box and finding our 1988 conversion story in the mess of contents strewn across the garage floor, Jonetta began her process of convincing me to make it public through the venue of a book. God's providence.

Why bring this up? Simply to give God the glory and credit for using *Muscle and a Shovel* to reach thousands of lost souls.

Friend, I take no credit for this! It is God alone who deserves every shred of fruit that has come from that humble work. *Muscle and a Shovel* was intended to reach the lost and perishing with the ancient gospel of Jesus Christ, and His bride, the church.

This story, *When Shovels Break*, is intended to reach the fallen and unfaithful with the message of hope and forgiveness that is found *only in* the gospel. It is intended to help restore those who were once baptized into Jesus Christ, but now find themselves in that horrible place of no fellowship, doubt, spiritual discouragement, and even sin. I am confident that this work will be as controversial as the first work, but let us pray that it will be a "positive" controversy.

This "preface" serves to bring you to the issue that I call, "A Great Cancer in the body of Jesus Christ." Brethren, this is a cancer that, if left untreated, will kill the church of our Lord. It will, in the least, continue to damage and cripple His body.

What is this great cancer eating away at the body of Christ here on earth? It has two components: gossip (slander; backbiting) and arrogance.

Nothing, in my humble opinion, has been more devastating, has broken more friendships, has caused more heartache and grief, has fostered more strife, has ran more brethren away from the church, and has given Satan the greatest foothold to destroy the body of Christ *from within* than gossip, slander, and backbiting. Add arrogance to the mix and Satan has a platform to work from.

Before you decide this chapter may no longer be worthy of your time, please give me the latitude to share some real-life results with you.

I started an experiment over two years ago that involved four people. Little did I know at the time that the experiment would eventually cover a span of two years and include over four hundred people.

The experiment was comprised of:

- Ten interview questions
- Four unfaithful members of the church of Christ.

I wanted to know why these four people became unfaithful and record the results.

I asked each one of the four to give me two names of unfaithful members that they knew personally. I tried to generate two new names from each interview, which is how this project grew to a little over four hundred.

It could have gone on, involving thousands, but I ended the experiment after interviewing a little over four hundred participants.

The interview started in Arkansas and eventually included unfaithful brethren from nine states. After countless hours writing emails, making phone calls, sending letters by US Mail, and meeting people in person, the results were shocking.

The participants simply had to meet two points of criteria:

1. Brethren who are known to have voluntarily become completely inactive in attendance at any location where the body of Christ meets regularly.

2. Brethren who, upon my contact, explanation, and inquiry, would be willing participants in allowing me to interview them with a series of questions relating to their past experience with the churches of Christ.

Although this is not a scientific poll, much was gleaned from these questions and the shocking results, in my opinion, need to be shared with the brotherhood.

I share these results not to beat up the church or to discourage the brethren, but because I love the church. I want my brothers and sisters in Christ to know some of the causes of unfaithfulness and how they can help those who have fallen away.

My passion is for the church of our Lord, to defend our brotherhood, and in no way criticize our brotherhood unduly. My love for the blood-bought church of Christ is deep, and is only matched by my sincere love for the brethren.

Regarding the experiment, I established control guidelines at the beginning of every interview in an effort to motivate participation and to receive the most *honest* feedback possible. The control guidelines were:

1. Names of participants and/or associated congregations would not be revealed in any form or fashion, neither verbally or in printed form.

2. Participant responses would be documented in written form, but identified only with a calendar date and state of residence.

3. Participant's information, personal or public, would not be shared with any person, person(s), organizations, or companies.

Some of those interviewed requested these control parameters in writing, so that they might have legal recourse in the event of any breach of agreement on my part, to which I happily complied.

Chapter 37
400 Interview Results

February 2015

Participant Questions and Results:

Question 1. Were you raised in the church or did you come out of a denomination?

Answer(s): Around 6 out of 10 unfaithful Christians stated that they had come out of a denomination. The remaining 4 grew up in the church.

Question 2. How long were you a faithful member?

Answer(s): After reviewing the data, it seems as though most of these unfaithful brethren left the church between 3 to 7 years after conversion. This data also *may* relate to our youth leaving the church between the ages of 18-25, but the theory is inconclusive.

Question 3. How long have you been inactive and/or away from fellowship/attendance?

Answer(s): The bulk of the data seemed to indicate that most of the participants had been inactive and away an average of 8-15 years. This points to the conclusion that most of the unfaithful had, at the time of their interview(s), been unfaithful *longer* than they were faithful.

Question 4.   From these four groups, Minister, Elders, Deacons, Members, which group or groups have made an attempt to help you return to the faith?

Answer(s):   This was the first "red flag" indicated in participant response. Approximately half of the respondents (approximately 5 out of 10) laughed at the question.

When I asked the reason for their reaction (laugh, smirk, etc.), approximately 3 out of the 5 who laughed stated that *no one* had inquired about their absence.

The other 2 out of 5 who laughed either answered in sarcastic replies, stated that they did not remember, or did not want to provide an answer.

The 5 out of 10 who answered the question without laughter: approximately 3 out of 5 stated

"Minister". The most common response of the remaining 2 out of 5 stated "Member".

The data seems to indicate that about 30% of the participants stated that no one had contacted them after their departure. Another 30% stated that the Minister had contacted them, and about 20% stated that a member had contacted them.

Question 5.   In your remembrance, how many times did those represented in the previous four groups attempt to help you return to the faith.

Answer(s):   The responses to this question indicated a second "red flag." Approximately 6 out of 10 replied, "Once." Approximately 2 of 10 replied, "twice." The remaining 2 of 10 did not know, did not remember, were unclear, gave no response or the responses varied wildly.

Question 6.   How have you been treated by faithful brethren since your departure?

Answer(s):   This question was extremely difficult to score, due to the subjection of individual opinions. Approximately 1 of 10 reported "strongly

negative." Approximately 3 of 10 reported
"negative." Approximately 2 of 10 reported
"same." The remaining 4 of 10 were so varied that
it was difficult to categorize.

Question 7.   If you can put the reason that you
have become unfaithful to the church of Christ into
one word, what would that word be?

Answer(s):   This response was weighted heavily
by a (my interpretation) response that pointed to a
common theme.

Between 7 and 8 out of the 10 respondents stated
"hypocrisy" in a variety of terms, phrases, and
words.

When asked to clarify, approximately 6 of 10 stated
the following in so many words, "gossip, mean-
spirited talk behind our back, fake, constant negative
talk about other people and/or other religions."

Between 1 and 2 out of the 10 respondents stated,
"Unable to make friends, too closed off to me, not

accepting of me." The remainder varied without a common thread or theme.

Question 8.   What would be a second reason that caused you to leave and/or causes you to remain in your current state relating to faithfulness?

Answer(s):   Between 5 and 6 out of 10 stated "arrogance" in a variety of terms, phrases, and words.

When asked to clarify, the same subset replied, "Snooty, too good for others, think they are better, made me feel like I wasn't as good as them, cocky, arrogant."

A further question regarding "arrogance" was implemented at this point: Which group caused you to have this feeling – Minister, Elders, Deacons, and/or Members?

Approximately 4 of 10 stated "Minister."

Approximately 2 of 10 stated "Minister and Elders."

Approximately 1 of 10 stated "Elders."

Approximately 1 of 10 stated "Members."

Approximately 1 of 10 reported no specific group but rather an over-arching *feeling* or *perception*.

The remaining 1 of 10 were either unsure or did not want to answer. None of the respondents stated that "Deacons" caused any negative feelings or perceptions. The responses of the remaining 4 or 5 answering this question were too varied and had no common theme.

Question 9.   What would be a third reason?

Answer(s):   A very small percentage of respondents successfully verbalized a third reason.

Question 10.   What would it take to bring you back to the Lord and His church?

Answer(s):   This final question was not as specific as it should have been, causing a plethora of differing responses. The only primary commonality I could establish within the participant responses is found within the following paraphrased summary; it is my opinion regarding the data fostered by Question 10 that the majority of the unfaithful desire friendship, acceptance, and a positive environment.

It may be important to note that it was in the rarest of cases to receive an answer whereby the individual took responsibility, or admitted personal culpability, for their own voluntary withdrawal from the fellowship.

This may simply confirm the principle of deflecting and imputing personal responsibility toward and onto others. It is difficult to quantify, but interesting to consider.

However, the data also demonstrates that the church is, at a minimum, *partially* responsible for a percentage (possibly a larger percentage that we would like to admit) of Christians who leave the faith.

This is the issue that we must address and repair. We must be honest with ourselves about the "cancer(s)" within the church of Christ and cure it before it is too late.

My faithful brother and sister in the Lord, gossip and arrogance gives the Adversary two legs to stand on. I do not stand as your judge, and I do not accuse you. My sincere hope and prayer is that all of us will remove the beam from our own eye. Will we take an honest look at our own hearts and motives?

If we love the Lord, we will work at following his commandments (see John 14:15; 1 John 2:3; 5:3), and the greatest of these is love (Matthew 22:36-40; 1 Corinthians 13:13).

Should we dismantle gossip? When Satan tempts us to gossip and malign others, why not remember our Lord's instructions – words that will destroy Satan's "leg" of gossip:

> *Moreover if thy brother shall trespass against thee, go and tell him his fault between thee and him alone: if he shall hear thee, thou hast gained thy brother* (Matthew 18:15).

God spoke to this issue long ago in Proverbs 16:28:

> *A perverse man sows strife, and a whisperer separates the best of friends* (NKJV).

The American Standard puts Proverbs 20:19 like this:

> *He that goeth about as a **tale-bearer** revealeth secrets; Therefore company not with him that openeth wide his lips.*

My mother used to say, "It is not gossip if it is true." I am so sorry to my mother for disagreeing, but the spreading of tales has nothing to do with truth. It cannot be much clearer than this:

> *But know this, that in the last days grievous times shall come. For men shall be lovers of self, lovers of money, boastful, haughty, railers, disobedient to parents, unthankful, unholy, without natural affection, implacable, **slanderers**, without self-control, fierce, no lovers of good, traitors, headstrong, puffed up, lovers of pleasure rather than lovers of God; holding a form of godliness, but having denied the power thereof. **From these also turn away*** (2 Timothy 3:1-5).

> *Having damnation, because they have cast off their first faith. And withal they learn to be idle, **wandering about from house to house; and not only idle, but tattlers also and busybodies, speaking things which they ought not*** (1 Timothy 5:12-13).

But let none of you suffer as a murderer, or as a thief, or as an evildoer, or as a **busybody in other men's matters** (1 Peter (4:15).

For we hear that there are some which walk among you disorderly, working not at all, **but are busybodies.** *Now them that are such we command and exhort by our Lord Jesus Christ, that with quietness they work, and eat their own bread* (2 Thessalonians 3:11-12).

Chapter 38
How Do You Come Back to God?
Step 1

It has been said that for every faithful follower of Christ, there are three that have fallen away. In other words, suppose that you attend a congregation of 150 people. This means that there are another 450 souls who have been baptized into Christ, began with great zeal, lost that zeal for whatever reason, and are now fallen away. And remember these are generally good, moral, hard-working, God-fearing, Jesus-believing people who have left the church.

Friend, if you find yourself among those who have left the faith, you *can* be forgiven! You *can*, once again, enjoy that peace that surpasses all understanding. You *can* again be an integral part of the Lord's mission. God *does* have a plan for you, and He, as hard as it may be to believe at this moment, *can* renew your hope and excitement for the faith of Jesus Christ!

Just know that this first step is the hardest step of all... **learning to forgive yourself.** Forgiving yourself requires a strong, conscious effort to put your sins in the past and forget them!

The Apostle Paul addressed this problem, but he also provided God's solution! Paul wrote,

> *Brethren, I count not myself to have apprehended:* **but this one thing I do, forgetting those things which are behind, and reaching forth unto those things which are before** (Philippians 3:13).

You also have to realize that there are unfortunately going to be those few brethren that seem to make it their job to remind you of your past sins. They are the few that will hold on to that grudge, and they will tirelessly remind everyone around you of your great unfaithfulness, desperately trying to prevent you from forgetting your past.

But here's what they do not know. No one – and I mean *no one* – hates your sins more than *you* do! I can admit to you that there is no brother or sister on earth that torments me daily for my past sins more than I do.

My brethren can gossip, back-bite, and hate me for my past sins, but the sum total of all of their retaliation does not come close to the daily torment executed upon my heart by my *own memory* of my past sins.

They *think* they are hurting me, and they are. However, my own mind hurts me *much* more. The guilt and shame of my past sins act as a whip and chain that seem to exist only to beat my heart with each day's sunrise. This is why we must hold fast to Paul's words of encouragement.

The daily pain and affliction caused to our minds over our past sins should help us remember that Jesus came for *us*. He came for *you*. Mark 2:16-17 says,

> *And when the scribes and Pharisees saw him eat with publicans and sinners, they said unto his disciples, How is it that he eateth and drinketh with publicans and sinners? When Jesus heard it, he saith unto them, They that are whole have no need of the physician, but they that are sick: I came not to call the righteous, but sinners to repentance.*

We often forget *who* it was that Jesus came for. Jesus came for the sick, not the healthy. Jesus broke bread with those who needed Him the most.

Those outside of Christ need to repent of their sins (Acts 3:19), make a public confession of their belief in Jesus (Acts 8:37), and be baptized for the remission of sins (Acts 2:38) to be put into Christ (Romans 6:3-6) and added by the Lord to His church (Acts 2:47).

We then spend our lives willingly walking in the light (Psalm 119:105; 1 John 1:7), until that day of our departure from this physical life (Revelation 2:10).

However, our loving and merciful Father has *also* given those, His children who have fallen away, a very clear path of return.

Children of God who have fallen away must also repent of our sins (Luke 15:18-19). God wants us to return to the light and to return to the fellowship of our brothers and sisters. John wrote,

> *But if we walk in the light, as he is in the*
> *light, we have fellowship one with another,*
> *and the blood of Jesus Christ his Son*
> *cleanseth us from all sin* (1 John 1:7).

God's Spirit, through John, reveals the cleansing principles so that we might once again bask in His continual cleansing from all sin: 1) walking in the light and 2) fellowshipping with one another.

Secondly, He declares with great specificity, how Christians who sin may find a cleansing from all unrighteousness,

*If we **confess our sins**, he is faithful and just to forgive us our sins, and to cleanse us from all unrighteousness* (1 John 1:9).

But who do we confess our sins to? The Bible interprets *itself* with consistent precision,

*Confess your faults **one to another, and pray one for another***, *that ye may be healed. The effectual fervent prayer of a righteous man availeth much* (James 5:16).

We do not confess to a "priest in a booth." We do not confess to a board or committee. We confess our faults *one to another*. In turn, we pray for one another. We do not beat those who are down and discouraged; we become encouragers and up-lifters of those who have fallen. This may be, in my opinion, one of the most neglected issues in our brotherhood.

Here's a good case-in-point. I know an elder who has, at several baptisms, said, "We'll never be as clean as we were the day we were baptized. It would be great if we could sit up in the balcony of the church building and shoot them with a high-powered rifle as soon as they come out of the water!"

This brother's perception is that those who are baptized should be killed as soon as they come up out of the water because, in his thinking, they will never be cleaner from sin.

As hard is this might be to believe, these are the verifiable words of an "elder." What a bleak, unbiblical, and spiritually incorrect attitude.

If his thinking is biblically correct, we should take his idea to the extreme. We should kill all newborn children as soon as they come out of the womb, so that they will never have the opportunity to grow to the knowledge of right and wrong, and have the potential to commit sin. What a preposterous thought.

Even the *most sinful* of God's children can be cleansed of all unrighteousness if they simply *obey* His instructions of grace and forgiveness. Even the most sinful among us can enjoy restoration in Christ and might just become one of the most *fruitful* of Christians!

When a sinful Christian falls to his (or her) knees in brokenness, shame, and complete regret, our Lord cleanses us of *all* unrighteousness (John 1:7-9). When we admit and confess our sins, He forgives us of everything!

His promise of forgiving us for all of our unrighteousness means that He does not and cannot pick and choose which sins to forgive and which sins to hold against us. It is an "all or nothing" deal, and God cannot lie (Titus 1:2).

God's promises are the only promises that you can bank on. Both Old and New Testaments are filled with stories of forgiveness and "second" chances.

Would you ask someone to do something that you are not willing to do yourself? Do you think God is any different? Jesus taught His followers a critical, foundational point when He said,

> *Ye have heard that it hath been said, Thou shalt love thy neighbor, and hate thine enemy. But I say unto you, Love your enemies, bless them that curse you, do good to them that hate you, and pray for them which despitefully use you, and persecute you; That ye may be the children of your Father which is in heaven: for he maketh his sun to rise on the evil and on the good, and sendeth rain on the just and on the unjust* (Matthew 5:43-45).

God does not ask you to do anything He is unwilling to do Himself. He is asking you to forgive. Forgive everyone, even your enemies!

This is what God has done. God loves His enemies. When you and I sin, we become God's enemies (Romans 8:7), but this in no way removes His love for us. Paul tells us,

> *But God commendeth his love toward us, in that, while we were yet sinners, Christ died for us. Much more then, being now justified by his blood, we shall be saved from wrath through him. For if, when we were enemies, we were reconciled to God by the death of his Son, much more, being reconciled, we shall be saved by his life. And not only so, but we also joy in God through our Lord Jesus Christ, by whom we have now received the atonement* (Romans 5:8-11).

I have, unfortunately, met a handful in our brotherhood who are so self-righteous that they appear to have lost any fiber of compassion or true Christian love. Their condescending attitudes speak volumes to all around, *"I am above you, because I am without sin."*

Jesus was the *only* man to have been without sin (Hebrews 4:15), yet *He*, in contrast to the previously mentioned brethren, was meek, lowly, compassionate, and loving.

These brethren would be well-served by remembering the woman caught in adultery,

> *Jesus went unto the mount of Olives. And early in the morning he came again into the temple, and all the people came unto him; and he sat down, and taught them.*

> *And the scribes and Pharisees brought unto him a woman taken in adultery; and when they had set her in the midst, They say unto him, Master, this woman was taken in adultery, in the very act. Now Moses in the law commanded us, that such should be stoned: but what sayest thou? This they said, tempting him that they might have to accuse him.*

> *But Jesus stooped down, and with his finger wrote on the ground, as though he heard*

them not. So when they continued asking
him, he lifted up himself, and said unto them,
He that is without sin among you, let him
first cast a stone at her.

And again he stooped down, and wrote on
the ground. And they which heard it, being
convicted by their own conscience, went out
one by one, beginning at the eldest, even
unto the last: and Jesus was left alone, and
the woman standing in the midst.

When Jesus had lifted up himself, and saw
none but the woman, he said unto her,
Woman, where are those thine accusers?
hath no man condemned thee? She said, No
man, Lord. And Jesus said unto her, Neither
do I condemn thee: go, and sin no more
(John 8:1-11).

God's grace and compassion are always
encompassed in the envelope of His command, *"Go and*
sin no more." This means that we *try our best.* Look at
Peter who wept over his own sins (i.e. quick temper,

violence, public denial of Christ three times), wept over his own sins, and never gave up. As a matter of fact, Peter would later preach the first gospel sermon ever preached to the entire house of Israel (Acts 2)!

Now, does this mean that we can live any way we want? God forbid! God's forgiveness is not a license to continue to run after sin, for Paul wrote, *"Shall we continue in sin, that grace may abound? God forbid!"* (Romans 6:1b-2a). God calls us to live holy lives (1 Thessalonians 4:7; 2 Timothy 1:9; 1 Peter 1:13-16), but friend, when we sin we have the Advocate Jesus Christ with the Father (1 John 2:1)!

God is ready, willing, and able to forgive you. He *desires* to forgive you! Isaiah said,

> *Let the wicked forsake his way, and the unrighteous man his thoughts: and let him return unto the LORD, and he will have mercy upon him; and to our God, for he will abundantly pardon* (Isaiah 55:7).

Brother or sister, I beg of you one thing: please do not limit the blood of Jesus Christ. Please do not allow the shame and guilt to flog your heart. Do not allow your regret and sorrow to define God's desire and ability to forgive you.

Begin by forgiving yourself. Won't you follow the path back to Him? It will only cost you a small amount of trust.

Chapter 39
Coming Back to God
Step 2

Let's be honest with each other. It's hard to forgive people, and no one has had to put up with the kind of unfair treatment you have received. No one has had to endure gossip, lies about their behavior, slander, betrayal, whispers, isolation, insults, arrogant "brethren," mean-spirited emails, "cold" shoulders in public, hatefulness, etc., like *you* have, right?

I know your feelings, because I have experienced all of these things just as you have. But let's *keep* being honest. Our sins have caused our retribution, and those Christians who have treated us this way are not perfect (even when they think they are).

We, sinful Christians, are willing to own our mistakes. Ownership of our sin leads us to the next step, forgiving those who have hurt and wounded us. Yes, Christian people will hurt and kill their wounded. It is a fact, but using this "excuse" doesn't hurt them; it hurts *you*.

Bitterness and your lack of being able to forgive those who have trespassed against you will put your soul into *the lake which burneth with fire and brimstone: which is the second death* (Revelation 21:8).

Yes, I agree. It's not fair, but it is just. God is a Holy and Just God. His forgiveness to you is contingent upon *your* forgiveness of others.

Jesus taught a parable that is critical for us who are struggling with forgiving those who have hurt us so much. He said,

> *Therefore is the kingdom of heaven likened unto a certain king, which would take account of his servants. And when he had begun to reckon, one was brought unto him, which owed him ten thousand talents.*
>
> *But forasmuch as he had not to pay, his lord commanded him to be sold, and his wife, and children, and all that he had, and payment to be made. The servant therefore fell down, and worshipped him, saying, Lord, have patience with me, and I will pay thee all. Then the lord of that servant was moved with compassion, and loosed him, and forgave him the debt.*

*But the same servant went out, and found
one of his fellow servants, which owed him
an hundred pence: and he laid hands on
him, and took him by the throat, saying,
Pay me that thou owest. And his fellow
servant fell down at his feet, and besought
him, saying, Have patience with me, and I
will pay thee all. And he would not: but
went and cast him into prison, till he
should pay the debt. So when his fellow
servants saw what was done, they were
very sorry, and came and told unto their
lord all that was done.*

*Then his lord, after that he had called him,
said unto him, O thou wicked servant, I
forgave thee all that debt, because thou
desiredst me: Shouldest not thou also have
had compassion on thy fellow servant, even
as I had pity on thee? And his lord was
wroth, and delivered him to the
tormentors, till he should pay all that was
due unto him.*

*So likewise shall my heavenly Father do
also unto you, if ye from your hearts
forgive not everyone his brother their
trespasses* (Matthew 18:23-35).

The thrust of this passage is found in verse 35, "So, likewise, shall God do to you." If you, from your heart, do not forgive everything that others have done to you, God **cannot** forgive you.

But doesn't our forgiveness have a limit? This was Peter's question in Matthew 18:21,

*...Lord, how oft shall my brother sin
against me, and I forgive him? Till seven
times* (Matthew 18:21)?

And our Lord's answer to Peter?

*Jesus saith unto him, I say not unto thee,
Until seven times: but, Until seventy times
seven* (v.22).

Now if you just grabbed your calculator, you missed His point completely! If you think that our Lord said that we can only forgive 490 times, you've missed it!

You are smarter than that. Isn't He teaching a fundamental principle of forgiveness? That our forgiveness towards those that repeatedly hurt us is to be always abounding and endless?

If God expects you to have endless forgiveness, are you really going to believe that God will *not* forgive you for the sins you've committed *after* your baptism?

Friend, your eternal hope depends on a simple decision to forgive those who have hurt you.

Chapter 40
Coming Back to God
Step 3

The primary thing that led me down the road to leaving the Lord and going back into sin was disappointment. I was disappointed when God did not give me everything I asked Him for in prayer. I was young, immature, and had not developed the proper, Bible-based expectations of prayer.

My mind said, "Whatever I ask of God will be given to me because I am a Christian." When God did not answer my prayers in the affirmative, I was disappointed.

Disappointment led to discouragement. "Does God really love me? Does He hear me? If God loves me then He will give me what I want!" This is a manipulation. "If you love me, then *prove* it by giving me what I want!" It is similar to the spoiled child trying to manipulate a parent using emotional bribery.

I read,

> *Ask, and it shall be given you; seek, and ye shall find; knock, and it shall be opened unto you: For every one that asketh receiveth; and he that seeketh findeth; and to him that knocketh it shall be opened* (Matthew 7:7-8).

"It's settled. God will give me whatever I pray for." This was my expectation. My messed-up expectation made God nothing more than a "genie in a bottle." He existed to grant my every wish, and if He did not give me my every request, then disappointment and discouragement followed.

Sister and brother, has this been a challenge in your life? If it has not, then I applaud you! If it has then let me try to help you.

Let's start with this. You and I realize that the scriptures must remain in their intended context for the Truth to be found and understood properly. There is a plethora of verses about prayer that, if taken out of context, create false expectations. For instance, look at Elijah's prayers about rain,

> *Elijah was a man subject to like passions as we are, and he prayed earnestly that it might not rain: and it rained not on the earth by the space of three years and six months. And he prayed again, and the heaven gave rain, and the earth brought forth her fruit* (James 5:17-18).

Does this mean that we can pray and expect God to adjust the weather according to our own desires? In our own mind it *can* mean exactly that, but only if we take these verses out of their intended context.

Have you ever been in a Bible study and heard someone say, "Well, *to me* this scripture means...?"

Whoa! Hold on, friend! This is a dangerous approach to interpreting scripture. The "to me this means" approach allows God's Word to *mean* something *different* to every reader, causing the Truth to be minimized, altered, twisted, and defined by the limited intellect and knowledge of the person reading the scripture.

This approach gives credence to the idea that God is an incompetent writer. Christians must take great care when reading the scriptures. We must put effort into allowing the Bible to interpret *itself*, rather than going down the path of "to me this means..."

Peter said,

> *Knowing this first, **that no prophecy of the scripture is of any private interpretation**. For the prophecy came*

not in old time by the will of man: but

holy men of God spake as they were

moved by the Holy Ghost (1 Peter 1:20-

21).

The Bible is not open to individual, private

interpretation. If we cannot use our own, personalized,

private interpretation, then what do we do?

We accept the fact that even the most uneducated

can understand the Bible. Paul said,

For we write none other things unto you,

than what ye read or acknowledge; and I

trust ye shall acknowledge even to the

end (2 Corinthians 1:13).

The New King James puts it this way,

For we are not writing any other things

*to you **than what you read or***

***understand**. Now I trust you will*

***understand**, even to the end.*

God has written His will into a Document that can

be understood by the common man. He is not a God of

confusion (1 Corinthians. 14:33). Paul confirmed this in

his letter to the church of Christ at Ephesus,

> *How that by revelation He made known*
> *to me the mystery (as I have briefly*
> *written already, by which, when you*
> *read,* ***you may understand my***
> ***knowledge in the mystery of Christ),***
> *which in other ages was not made known*
> *to the sons of men, as it has now been*
> *revealed by the Spirit to His holy*
> *apostles and prophets* (Ephesians 3:3-5,
> NKJV).

You *can* understand the Bible, but a proper
understanding comes through a willingness to study the
Bible in its context. What does that mean? That means
that we study *all* of the scriptures relating to a specific
topic, such as prayer and the proper expectations of
prayer, and keep them in God's intended context.

Building biblically correct expectations of prayer
can be summarized by Christ's prayer in the Garden of
Gethsemane. Look at what the Lord said in His prayer to
God regarding His fear and anxiety when He was about to
be crucified,

> *Then Jesus came with them to a place*
> *called Gethsemane, and said to the*

disciples, Sit here while I go and pray over there. And He took with Him Peter and the two sons of Zebedee, and He began to be sorrowful and deeply distressed. Then He said to them, My soul is exceedingly sorrowful, even to death. Stay here and watch with Me.

*He went a little farther and fell on His face, and prayed, saying, O My Father, if it is possible, let this cup pass from Me; nevertheless, **not as I will, but as You will**.*

Then He came to the disciples and found them asleep, and said to Peter, What? Could you not watch with Me one hour? Watch and pray, lest you enter into temptation. The spirit indeed is willing, but the flesh is weak.

Again, a second time, He went away and prayed, saying, O My Father, if this cup

cannot pass away from Me unless I drink
it, **Your will be done.**

And He came and found them asleep
again, for their eyes were heavy. So He
left them, went away again, and prayed
the third time, **saying the same words**
(Matthew 26:36-44).

Brother and sister, you may think that what I am about to say is elementary, and possibly too *simple* for your consideration, but my sincere prayer is that you embrace the simplicity of what I am about to say.

Proper expectations of prayer depends on your acceptance of the fact that *God's* will must always come before *your* will, and that your prayers need to align with God's will. It is as simple as saying, "Father, you know what is best for me, so please do what *you* know is best for me, my family, and our future."

God's will, His wisdom, His decisions, and His plans for you are superior to your wisdom, your decisions, and your plans for yourself.

Isaiah 55:8 says,

> *For my thoughts are not your thoughts,*
> *neither are your ways my ways, saith the*
> *LORD. For as the heavens are higher*
> *than the earth, so are my ways higher*
> *than your ways, and my thoughts than*
> *your thoughts.*

John wrote,

> *These things I have written to you who*
> *believe in the name of the Son of God,*
> *that you may know that you have eternal*
> *life, and that you may continue to believe*
> *in the name of the Son of God. Now this*
> *is the confidence that we have in Him,*
> ***that if we ask anything according to His***
> ***will, He hears us*** (1 John 5:13-14).

It can't be that easy, can it? Yes, it is that easy.
Remember, God is too good to be cruel, and He is too
wise to make a mistake. Second, God knows your every
need even before you do. Jesus said,

> *Therefore do not be like them. For your*
> *Father knows the things you have need of*
> *before you ask Him* (Matthew 6:8).

Doesn't this give you goose-bumps? God knows the things you need before you ask Him! But the operative word is "need." God supplies our needs, not our extravagant desires. *"And my God shall supply **all your need** according to His riches in glory by Christ Jesus"* (Philippians 4:19).

You know this is true in your own life. Suppose your daughter comes to you and says, "Dad/Mom, I need a car."

"Honey, I've known that you've needed a car for some time now," you reply.

"Ok, I want a new Lexus," she demands.

"A Lexus?" you respond with a laugh. "Wouldn't you be thankful for a car that *I* think is more suitable for you at this point in your life?" You ask.

"No! I want a new Lexus!" she demands.

"Well," you explain in a calm and loving manner, "I know you need a car and I will provide a good car for you, but the car you receive will be compatible with your current needs."

You provide your daughter a used Chevy Malibu. Is she humble, grateful, and sincerely appreciative? Or is she disappointed, ungrateful, and resentful?

Do we appreciate how God has met our every need? Do we thank Him for His love and provision, even when we are undeserving?

Brother or sister, if you inhale a breath of air, it is God's air. If you take a drink of water, it is God's water. If you go outside and stand in the dirt, it is God's dirt.

The very fact that you have life in your body is entirely because God has given you life. He has given you everything because of and through Jesus Christ. It is written,

> For **by him** [Jesus] *were all things created, that are in heaven, and that are in earth, visible and invisible, whether they be thrones, or dominions, or principalities, or powers: all things were created by him, and for him: And he is before all things,* **and by him all things consist** (Colossians 1:16-17).

Your existence is literally by and through Jesus Christ. You live within the palm of God's hand, and you owe your existence to Jesus Christ. Realizing our great debt to Jesus Christ should be a motivator toward beginning to forgive those who have sinned against us.

Chapter 41
Coming Back to God
Step 4

How do you deal with your disappointments? What if God uses our disappointments to our future benefit?

Paul, an apostle of God, wrote about being disappointed,

> *And our hope for you is steadfast, because we know that as you are partakers of the sufferings, so also you will partake of the consolation.* **For we do not want you to be ignorant, brethren, of our trouble which came to us in Asia: that we were burdened beyond measure, above strength, so that we despaired even of life** (1 Corinthians 1:7-8).

Paul was in dire straits. His life had been in jeopardy. He faced one of the worst situations a man (or woman) can face. There's little doubt that this man understood the meaning of disappointment.

He had given up everything: his prestige among the Jews, his high-level education, his authority and power, and his future career – all to follow Jesus Christ.

And following Jesus Christ had put his own *life* in peril. Do you think Paul understood the meaning of disappointment and discouragement? There can be no doubt!

But Paul, inspired by the Holy Spirit, revealed something incredible! He revealed that this "peril" had a *purpose*! He went on to write,

> *Yes, we had the sentence of death in ourselves,* **that we should not trust in ourselves but in God** *who raises the dead, who delivered us from so great a death, and does deliver us;* **in whom we trust that He will still deliver us**, *you also helping together in prayer for us, that thanks may be given by many persons on our behalf for the gift granted to us through many* (2 Corinthians 1:7-11).

Friend, it is about your reaction. We, Christians who have fallen into sin and who are considering whether or not to come back to God, will react in one of two ways: we see our current position as an opportunity to place our trust in Him, or we use our current status as an opportunity to resent and reject Him.

How can God reach *you*? Sometimes hard-headed people are hard to reach. If life is smooth, easy, comfortable, and without any real struggle, would we ever need to come to God?

Is it possible that we are allowed to come to places in our lives whereby we find that need for God?

There was a man who lived long ago. He was a child of God. God had a purpose for the man, but the man ran away from God and God's presence. The man put many others in peril by running away from God. Then he found himself facing death in a horrible place. He, facing death, cried out to God for rescue. God heard his prayers and saved the man's life (Jonah 1-2).

God has a purpose for your life (1 Corinthians 12:8-13). When you and I run from that purpose, we can find ourselves in perilous straits. We can, and often do, put others in danger, even damaging *them* along the way.

When we find ourselves away from the presence of God, we are in real trouble, even when the seas are calm. When we've been disappointed in our Christian life, what was the real cause of our disappointment? Does God *really* want you to be in pain and anguish, or is this that opportunity that you've needed to cry out to Him?

Chapter 42
Coming Back to God
Step 5

We all need a "Jonathan," not a "John." People need people; we need a true friend. God saw that Adam was alone (Genesis 2:18), so he created a soul-mate, a helper, a companion, a wife, and a true friend.

It has been said that a man is not an island unto himself. It is a phrase that expresses one's need for a connection to others.

Every man and woman needs a true friend. Why? Because we have been made in the likeness of God, and God was not *alone*. God said in Genesis 1:26,

> *Let **Us** make man in **Our** image,*
> *according to **Our** likeness; let them have*
> *dominion over the fish of the sea, over*
> *the birds of the air, and over the cattle,*
> *over all the earth and over every*
> *creeping thing that creeps on the earth.*

God has made us to be *social* beings; therefore, we have an inherent need to be social, to be connected with another human being. Our Lord not only understood this need, He acted upon it,

> *And He called the twelve to Himself, and*
> *began to send them out **two by two**, and*

gave them power over unclean spirits
(Mark 6:7).

Jesus is the Master. He had a variety of options at His disposal. He was God in flesh, so He had all knowledge. This shows that Jesus knew that companionship was necessary for both Himself and His followers. Jesus knew the importance of having a true friend.

You need a true friend. A true friend is not a friend who participates in your sins. A true friend is not a friend who enables you or remains silent when you sin. A true friend is someone who loves you enough to encourage you toward doing the right thing. A true friend loves you enough that they will speak up when they think you are going down the wrong path.

This is the kind of friend *you* need. Search for and pursue this type of friend. Many times friends like this can be found within your family, the family of God.

The Bible says that David had a friend named Jonathan, and that their souls were knit together. Jonathan loved David as his own soul (1 Samuel 18:1). The latter part of Proverbs 18:24 says that there is a friend that sticks closer than a brother.

Ecclesiastes 4:9-12 makes a powerful argument for
the need of a friend,

> *Two are better than one; because they*
> *have a good reward for their labour. For*
> *if they fall, the one will lift up his fellow:*
> *but woe to him that is alone when he*
> *falleth; for he hath not another to help him*
> *up. Again, if two lie together, then they*
> *have heat: but how can one be warm*
> *alone? And if one prevail against him, two*
> *shall withstand him; and a threefold cord*
> *is not quickly broken.*

Like David, you need the *right* kind of friend.
Paul warned in 1 Corinthians 15:33,

> *Do not be deceived: Evil company corrupts*
> *good habits* (NKJV).

The need for a good and true friend is vital to the
life of the Christian and the health of the soul. Jesus said,

> *Greater love hath no man than this, that a*
> *man lay down his life for his friends* (John
> 15:13).

Chapter 43
God's Awesome Love
And Grace

Brother and sister, you *can* step back into God's love and grace. Without God's love and grace, we are, of all men, most miserable; our condition is hopeless. Paul said,

> *But if there be no resurrection of the dead, then is Christ not risen: And if Christ be not risen, then is our preaching vain, and your faith is also vain. Yea, and we are found false witnesses of God; because we have testified of God that he raised up Christ: whom he raised not up, if so be that the dead rise not. For if the dead rise not, then is not Christ raised: And if Christ be not raised, your faith is vain; ye are yet in your sins. Then they also which are fallen asleep in Christ are perished. If in this life only we have hope in Christ, we are of all men most miserable* (1 Corinthians 15:13-19).

Without Jesus Christ and His resurrection, we have no hope. However, we know that Jesus Christ was raised from the dead! How can we know this without a shadow of a doubt? The volumes of scriptural information we have about Jesus Christ, combined with secular history, and archeology should be enough, but I want to visit another aspect that lends to the unmatched credibility of the gospel: eye witness testimony.

Consider the US Constitution, Article III, Section 3, Clause 1:

```
Treason against the `United States,
shall consist only in levying war
against them, or in adhering to their
enemies, giving them aid and comfort.
No person shall be convicted of
Treason unless on the testimony of two
witnesses to the same overt act, or on
confession in open court.
```

Two witnesses, according to our Constitution, can convict a person of treason. Imagine what 500 witnesses could do. With this in mind, consider the inspired apostle's words,

Moreover, brethren, I declare unto you the gospel which I preached unto you, which also ye have received, and wherein ye stand; By which also ye are saved, if ye

*keep in memory what I preached unto you,
unless ye have believed in vain. For I
delivered unto you first of all that which I
also received, how that Christ died for our
sins according to the scriptures; And that
he was buried, and that he rose again the
third day according to the scriptures:* **And
that he** [Jesus Christ] **was seen of Cephas,
then of the twelve:** *After that,* **he was seen
of above five hundred brethren at once;** *of
whom the greater part remain unto this
present, but some are fallen asleep* (1
Corinthians 15:1-6).

Yes, you can be sure that Jesus Christ is the Risen
Savior. Therefore, you can trust in His promises. This
means that you can trust in God's grace for *you*. Paul, in
this same chapter, said,

*For I am the least of the apostles, that am
not meet to be called an apostle,* **because I
persecuted the church of God. But by the
grace of God I am what I am:** *and his
grace which was bestowed upon me was
not in vain; but I laboured more*

> *abundantly than they all: yet not I, but the*
> *grace of God which was with me* (1
> Corinthians 15:9-10).

Friend, I've written all of this to bring you to the most important fact affecting you and your future: the magnitude of God's love for you. This same Paul, a man who had previously persecuted the church of Christ, explains the great love and grace,

> *But God, who is rich in mercy, for his*
> *great love wherewith he loved us, Even*
> *when we were dead in sins, hath quickened*
> *us together with Christ, (by grace ye are*
> *saved;) And hath raised us up together,*
> *and made us sit together in heavenly*
> *places in Christ Jesus: That in the ages to*
> *come he might shew the exceeding riches*
> *of his grace in his kindness toward us*
> *through Christ Jesus. For by grace are ye*
> *saved through faith; and that not of*
> *yourselves: it is the gift of God* (Ephesians
> 2:4-8).

You are a Christian, so you know that Paul is not teaching "faith only" salvation in these passages. His point is the deep mercy, great love, and the riches of God's grace for us who are Christians.

Even though we, every one of us, have sinned and do sin (Romans 3:23; 1 John 1:8, 10), God made us alive together with Christ (Romans 6:3-5; Galatians 3:26-27), thereby saving us by His grace (Ephesians 2:5).

The location of God's incredible grace is found within Jesus Christ (Ephesians 1:3), and when a sinful Christian trusts God enough to obey His commands and they follow through in active obedience, that Christian is restored to a position inside God's wonderful grace.

Having this biblical knowledge helps us tremendously toward coming back to the Lord. But those who fall away and later return have an underlying fear. It is the fear of falling away *again*.

How do we keep from falling away again? The answer is in the Bible and it is amazing!

Chapter 44
The Faithful Interviewed:
Shocking Results

Ego Board
Attendance Faith
Church-Building-Evangelism

Brethren will say after your baptism, "Now all you've got to do is be faithful unto death," referring to Revelation 2:10. Sounds easy, right?

The real problem with this statement is that it is rarely ever followed with, "And here's *how* you stay faithful unto death." Revelation 2:10 is usually followed with a reference to Hebrews 10:25 in an effort to make the new convert understand how missing a service means *unfaithfulness.*

While these thoughts and scriptural references are honorable, well-intentioned, instructive, and completely relevant, quoting these two verses to the new convert does not mean we no longer have any personal responsibility to that new babe in Christ. Many good brethren seem to think that telling them to be faithful in attendance after baptism is the end of the church's responsibility; and later they wonder *why* the newly converted Christian fell away.

Just be here three times a week, check off your scorecard, and you'll be fine, is the unspoken message. I have searched the scriptures for many years in an attempt to find this unspoken doctrinal message, but "attend three times a week" isn't there. New Testament Christians living in the first century had a level of love, appreciation for God, and a zeal for their faith that motivated them to meet *daily*.

Now, am I suggesting that our attendance is ***not*** important? **God forbid**! I am simply saying that we are avoiding our responsibility to feed the sheep when we say, "Just be here when you're supposed to be here, *and you'll make it to Heaven*" – or when we *act* like attendance is all that is required.

I have found, through a great deal of experience, that a shocking number of brethren who attend *every* service struggle secretly with sin. These "faithful" brethren have doubts about their faith and suffer tremendous guilt over their lack of zeal for the Lord and His church.

I have interviewed scores of brethren who are considered to be faithful, all in an effort to find out why the body of our Lord suffers and is in decline. The answers are nothing short of astounding!

Here are some of the questions and the most common responses from our "faithful" brethren.

Q: Do the elders know of your struggles?

A: Approximately 9 out of 10 replied: No.

Q: Why do the elders *not* know about your struggles?

A: The answers varied from person to person, but the three most common answers were: 1) They do not ask. 2) Our leadership tends to gossip. 3) Fear of judgment and/or being labeled.

Q: Why do you attend all three services each week?

A: 1) I'm supposed to be there. 2) The Bible says so. 3) I don't want to be judged as unfaithful by the others. 4) I don't want to go to Hell.

Q: On a scale from 1 to 10 with 10 being the highest, where do you rate your zeal for the church and for sharing the gospel with the lost?

A: Approximately 80% answered 5 or below. The remainder of responses averaged a score of 6. Scores of 7 – 10 were so rare that it was difficult to measure.

Q: Why, in your personal opinion, did you score yourself so low regarding your zeal?

A: The two most common responses were: 1) Fear. 2) I don't want the ones I bring to feel the way I do.

Is it possible that these answers represent an overarching "pulse" of the Lord's body today? I have spent time researching the condition, the thoughts, the concerns, and the perceptions of many in our brotherhood all over the country. Perhaps it is more prevalent than we know?

We, as a brotherhood, do recognize these issues. We even verbalize the problems in statements like: "membership is down," "we're doing good to maintain what we have," "brethren are apathetic in spreading the gospel," "or, that congregation seems dead."

Brethren, it begins with the "ego board." What is the ego board? It is that board that hangs in every congregation's building that lists the attendance numbers and contribution amount.

The ego board portrays an unbiblical focus and infers that attendance and money are the church's primary concerns. Consider our first century brethren. Their focus was three-fold:

1) Make disciples by spreading the gospel

2) Minister to the poor and needy among us

3) Build-up and encourage one another

There are simply too many scriptural references to list that establish, prove, support, and advocate these facts. With that being said, what if we posted the number of seeds sown the previous week instead of our attendance numbers? What if we posted the amount of money distributed to the poor, needy, and widows among us *rather* than the amount collected in last week's offering?

How would this affect the congregation's priorities, concerns, and zeal?

Recently I shared this idea with an older brother in Christ, and he was appalled!

"You can't suggest something like that," he responded in disgust, stepping to the cusp of anger.

"Why not?" I asked.

"That's not scriptural!" he said to me as if I were some half-baked extreme liberal.

Brother and sister, I want you to give his response your most honest and serious consideration. In this brother's mind, our long-held tradition (a tradition of men) of posting the attendance and contribution numbers is somehow the biblical *model*. Our current practice of posting these weekly stats was, in his mind, sanctioned, authorized, and even suggested within God's sacred text. But the idea of posting the total gospel seeds sown and the distribution of last week's collection is somehow not *scriptural*? Why not? Is it because it puts the focus on the spiritual health of the congregation rather than the numerical health? I will let you think about that for yourself.

While adjusting the ego board may not be a viable proposal, we must prayerfully evaluate why the church of our Lord is suffering and in decline in our contemporary society – especially within this country.

Brethren, we have long been guilty of "attendance faith" and "church building evangelism," and neither is working well for the Lord and His Cause.

The shepherds (Elders) call the sheep to the barn (church building). The sheep who show up are considered whole and healthy (attendance faith), while the missing sheep are, in *some* cases, being neglected by all of us.

We *invite* the lost to our building (church-building-evangelism) to meet our nice brethren and hear our fantastic preacher. When those invited do not show, we say to ourselves, "We did our job."

I ask you this honest question with complete humility, where do we find this in the New Testament? Can we find a single example, instruction, command, inference, idea, or even the *principle* of the idea of *inviting the lost* to worship taught anywhere in the New Testament? We simply cannot find this concept in the Bible.

We do, however, find that the saved went out into the world, shared the gospel message, and made converts by baptizing them into the Lord.

The saved would then follow in meeting together for worship, because worship offered to God is offered by those who have been saved. Brethren, this is the Bible's model.

Chapter 45
Never Falling Again:
God's Plan of Prevention

The Power of God's Instructions

How do we, as individual members of the Lord's body, cure these problems of sin, doubt, gossip, fear and apathy? And how do we, once restored, keep from falling away again?

In my opinion, and it is only an opinion, the answer can be found in 2 Peter. Consider God's words found in 2 Peter 1:10-11,

> *Wherefore the rather, brethren, give diligence to make your calling and election sure: for if ye do these things, ye shall never fall: For so an entrance shall be ministered unto you abundantly into the everlasting kingdom of our Lord and Savior Jesus Christ.*

Giving diligence prevents apathy. When we invest our time and energy into *doing* something, our apathy evaporates.

What are we to give diligence to? Making our calling and election sure. God, in this way, gives us *direction and purpose*. When we have direction and purpose, we become excited. Our zeal tends to grow from our focus on our purpose.

In these two verses we also find the answer to the question, "How can I keep from falling away again?" Peter said, *"For if ye do these things, ye shall **never** fall."*

Additionally, doing these things fosters *an entrance ministered unto us abundantly into the everlasting kingdom.*

Wow! God is revealing a specific "program," if you will, that destroys apathy, gives us direction and purpose, restores zeal, and will prevent us from falling away again. So what *are* these things Peter mentions?

The apostle Peter outlines *these things* in verses 5-7,

>*And beside this, giving all diligence, add to your faith virtue; and to virtue knowledge; And to knowledge temperance; and to temperance patience; and to patience godliness; And to godliness brotherly kindness; and to brotherly kindness charity. (2 Peter 1:5-7)*

We brothers and sisters in Christ can easily forget the goal that we are to strive for – the goal of pursuing, developing, and mastering Christ's virtues.

God's Spirit, through Peter, gave each Christian man and woman a plan for spiritual success in this life which will lead to our ultimate spiritual success – eternal life.

Call it a program, a blueprint, a syllabus, a game-plan, a living strategy. Call it whatever you like. God's instructions in verses 5-7 provide us with a series of goals that, if pursued, will give us the greatest rewards known to mankind. No other plan in the history of mankind contains this type of power and promise.

Notice the promised result of your willingness to follow God's simple life-plan,

> *For **if** these things be in you, and abound, they make you that ye shall neither be barren nor unfruitful in the knowledge of our Lord Jesus Christ* (2 Peter 1:8).

In contrast, Peter tells us about those who lack these things,

> *But he that lacketh these things is blind, and cannot see afar off, and **hath forgotten that he was purged from his old sins*** (2 Peter 1:9).

When we do *not* pursue these things, we fall into spiritual need. Then we risk forgetting that we were purged from our old sins.

Do you know what happens when we forget that we have been purged from our old sins? Discouragement, guilt, depression, fear, doubt. We might even resurrect that old man of sin.

When we don't pursue these things (virtue, knowledge, temperance, patience, Godliness, brotherly kindness, charity), or when we don't know our need to follow this spiritual instruction, we become blind – spiritually blind. We can't see *afar off*. Spiritual blindness is a scary and dangerous thing.

However, when we pursue these things, evil is overcome. Gossip is eradicated. Fear is flushed away. Discouragement is replaced with hope and excitement. Guilt is replaced with that peace that surpasses all understanding. Our doubt transforms into a humble confidence in God's promises, and "John," that old man of sin that was previously "us," remains buried. What wonderful news! When our shovel breaks, God's faith-building plan is the cure.

> *And beside this, giving all diligence, add to*
> *your faith virtue; and to virtue knowledge;*
> *And to knowledge temperance; and to*
> *temperance patience; and to patience*

godliness; And to godliness brotherly kindness; and to brotherly kindness charity.

Christians need purpose. We need something to strive for. Our faith is not about becoming professional "meeting attenders," it is about something far deeper. Our faith should shape and develop us, giving us peace, joy, and purpose for our life.

Our Christian life is meant to shape the future of our entire family as well as those generations to come. Our faith is meant to change all who are around us. The gospel changes everything it contacts into something better. God's Word does not return unto Him void (Isaiah 55:11).

Brother and sister, this is God's plan for your life, and it is a thrilling life of love, grace, purpose and passion. But as they say, Rome wasn't built overnight, right? How do you eat an elephant? One bite at a time. Let's look at the first building block...

Chapter 46
Never Falling Again:
God's Plan of Prevention

Virtue

Peter tells us to add virtue to our faith. In other words, add moral excellence to your faith. Bible texts help us to get a better understanding of virtue. Proverbs 3:1-3 says,

> *My son, forget not my law; but let thine heart keep my commandments: for length of days, and long life, and peace, shall they add to thee. Let not mercy and truth forsake thee: bind them about thy neck; write them upon the table of thine heart:*

How do you add virtue to your faith? Adding virtue requires an effort that involves both the head and the heart. *"Let thine heart keep my commandments."* When a sincere Christian makes an individual commitment to add virtue to their faith, the commitment begins with a heart-felt conviction, a passionate desire to make virtue a part of their faith.

Successfully adding virtue to your faith also requires your mind. Paul explains how we add virtue using our mind,

> *Whatsoever things are true, whatsoever things are honest, whatsoever things are just, whatsoever things are pure,*

> *whatsoever things are lovely, whatsoever things are of good report; if there be any virtue, and if there be any praise, **think** on **these** things.*

Our *thinking* is the key. God said, *"For as he thinketh in his heart, so is he"* (Proverbs 23:7). What we think in our mind also comes from our heart, and God said that our *thinking* determines who we are and what we become.

Jesus brilliantly validates this principle in Matthew 15:17-20,

> *Do not ye yet understand, that whatsoever entereth in at the mouth goeth into the belly, and is cast out into the draught? But those things which proceed **out of the mouth come forth from the heart**; and they defile the man. For out of the heart proceed evil thoughts, murders, adulteries, fornications, thefts, false witness, blasphemies: These are the things which defile a man: but to eat with unwashen hands defileth not a man.*

Chapter 47

Never Falling Again:
God's Plan of Prevention

Knowledge

The faith of the Lord Jesus Christ is a faith based on *knowledge.* It is a faith of one reasonable, rational, logical, and understandable Truth.

God, through Hosea, said,

> *My people are destroyed for lack of knowledge: because thou hast rejected knowledge, I will also reject thee, that thou shalt be no priest to me: seeing thou hast forgotten the law of thy God, I will also forget thy children* (Hosea 4:6).

Christians need knowledge – knowledge of the Bible. We are to study to show ourselves approved unto God (2 Timothy 2:15). We need knowledge so that Satan does not gain an advantage over us due to our ignorance (2 Corinthians 2:11).

Bible knowledge increases our faith and preserves us from falling into the corruption of the world. Our need for this knowledge is vital also because we cannot self-guide our lives into Heaven. Jeremiah said,

> *O LORD, I know that the way of man is not in himself: it is not in man that walketh to direct his steps* (10:23).

God's Word is Truth (John 17:17). It is the lamp that lights our path (Psalm 119:105), and it is the one Great Document that is able to make us complete and thoroughly equipped for every good work (2 Timothy 3:16-17).

God said that it is not good to be without knowledge (Proverbs 19:2). Paul, in talking about the Jews, said,

> *Brethren, my heart's desire and prayer to God for Israel is, that they might be saved. For I bear them record that they have a zeal of God, but not according to knowledge. For they being ignorant of God's righteousness, and going about to establish their own righteousness, have not submitted themselves unto the righteousness of God* (Romans 10:1-3).

It has been said that knowledge is power. I strongly disagree. It is the *application* of knowledge that holds power. Apply Bible knowledge to your life, and God through His power will bless you exceedingly!

Chapter 48

Never Falling Again:
God's Plan of Prevention

Temperance

The word *temperance* in the Bible comes from a Greek word that means "to master something," or "mastery" towards complete control over yourself (temptations, desires, and behavior).

The apostle eloquently outlined the battle between our mind and the flesh in Romans,

> *For that which I do I allow not: for what I would, that do I not; but what I hate, that do I. If then I do that which I would not, I consent unto the law that it is good. Now then it is no more I that do it, but sin that dwelleth in me. For I know that in me (that is, in my flesh,) dwelleth no good thing: for to will is present with me; but how to perform that which is good I find not. For the good that I would I do not: but the evil which I would not, that I do. Now if I do that I would not, it is no more I that do it, but sin that dwelleth in me* (7:15-20).

What a remarkable confession. This **apostle** admitted that he wanted to do right, but ended up doing what he hated! Paul admitted to his brethren at Rome that he sinned; however, he remained focused on the goal,

> *Brethren, I count not myself to have*
> *apprehended: but this one thing I do,*
> *forgetting those things which are behind,*
> *and reaching forth unto those things*
> *which are before, I press toward the*
> *mark for the prize of the high calling of*
> *God in Christ Jesus* (Philippians 3:13-
> 14).

Paul's words to the church of Christ at Philippi reveal at least 4 things:

1. His acknowledgement that he had not achieved spiritual perfection on this earth
2. His conscious effort to forget his past
3. His focus on the eternal goal
4. His pursuit of the eternal reward

Paul said,

> *But put ye on the Lord Jesus Christ, and*
> *make not provision for the flesh, to fulfill*
> *the lusts thereof* (Romans 13:14).

He said in 1 Corinthians 9:27,

> *But I keep under my body, and bring it*
> *into subjection: lest that by any means,*

> *when I have preached to others, I myself*
> *should be a castaway.*

The American Standard Version says,

> *but I buffet my body, and bring it into*
> *bondage: lest by any means, after that I*
> *have preached to others, I myself should*
> *be rejected (Ibid).*

Paul pressed toward the reward by denying his
fleshly desires. How? By bringing his body into the
subjection of his mind. He buffeted his body, bringing it
into bondage.

Paul didn't allow his body to enslave his mind, as
the world teaches, which is *do what feels good.* He put
effort into making his mind the master over his body.

Jesus demonstrated perfect temperance (self-control)
in Matthew 4:1-11,

> *Then was Jesus led up of the Spirit into the*
> *wilderness to be tempted of the devil. And*
> *when he had fasted forty days and forty*
> *nights, he was afterward an hungered.*
>
> *And when the tempter came to him, he*
> *said, If thou be the Son of God, command*

that these stones be made bread. But he answered and said, It is written, Man shall not live by bread alone, but by every word that proceedeth out of the mouth of God.

Then the devil taketh him up into the holy city, and setteth him on a pinnacle of the temple, And saith unto him, If thou be the Son of God, cast thyself down: for it is written, He shall give his angels charge concerning thee: and in their hands they shall bear thee up, lest at any time thou dash thy foot against a stone. Jesus said unto him, It is written again, Thou shalt not tempt the Lord thy God.

Again, the devil taketh him up into an exceeding high mountain, and sheweth him all the kingdoms of the world, and the glory of them; And saith unto him, All these things will I give thee, if thou wilt fall down and worship me. Then saith Jesus unto him, Get thee hence, Satan: for it is written, Thou shalt worship the Lord thy God, and him only shalt thou serve. Then the devil leaveth him, and, behold, angels came and ministered unto him.

Our Lord knows that our spirit is willing, but our flesh is weak (Matthew 26:41). Temperance requires desire and daily commitment. It takes practice, but like everything else, the more you practice self-control, the stronger your self-control becomes.

Chapter 49
Never Falling Again:
God's Plan of Prevention

Patience

> *Truly my soul waiteth upon God: from him*
> *cometh my salvation* (Psalm 62:1).

We want a faster Internet, a faster car, and a faster way to communicate. From the delivery of our food to flying around the world, speed drives a large part of our lives.

As technology grows, it becomes more dominant in our daily lives. The technology that serves us in such positive ways contains hidden, detrimental effects on our minds. It conditions us to be impatient.

When our Internet pages won't load, when traffic grinds to a slow pace, or when we have to wait more than five minutes at the drive-thru, we become anxious and agitated. Instant gratification is becoming the norm.

The anxiety generated by impatience is a big business in today's world. Prescriptions for anti-anxiety medications are at an all-time high, and they are expected to do nothing but increase in the coming years.

Why has God placed such a premium on patience? Because patience does something powerful for your faith. Patience has a job to do on your heart and mind. James wrote,

> *But let patience have her perfect work, that ye may be perfect and entire, wanting nothing* (1:4).

Patience molds you into a Christian who enjoys peace over anxiety. It develops you into a *perfect* man or woman of God. This does not imply that you will live a perfect life by never coming short of the glory of God, but rather that you are fully instructed and completely grounded in the faith of our Lord Jesus Christ. The perfect work of patience is the final reward at the end of a life lived in devotion to Christ.

How is patience developed? In many cases patience is shaped through struggles, trials, temptations, and persecution. James said,

> *My brethren, count it all joy when ye fall into divers temptations; knowing this, that the trying of your faith worketh patience* (1:2-3).

The temptations and trials of our faith work patience, and these verses should serve to shift our thinking about our own trials. When our faith is tested, we should be thankful to God rather than allowing fear, anxiety, and frustration to take over our mind.

What is the first step?

> *Be still, and know that I am God: I will be*
> *exalted among the heathen, I will be*
> *exalted in the earth. The LORD of hosts is*
> *with us; the God of Jacob is our refuge*
> (Psalm 46:10).

Know that God loves you and He is your refuge.
You have nothing to fear.

Psalm 130:5-6 says,

> *I wait for the LORD, my soul doth wait,*
> *and in his word do I hope. My soul waiteth*
> *for the Lord more than they that watch for*
> *the morning: I say, more than they that*
> *watch for the morning.*

The Psalmist learned to wait on God and to look to
God's Word for hope.

Isaiah 30:18 says,

> *And therefore will the LORD wait, that he*
> *may be gracious unto you, and therefore*
> *will he be exalted, that he may have mercy*
> *upon you: for the LORD is a God of*
> *judgment: blessed are all they that wait for*
> *him.*

Patience demonstrates a deep trust in God and His decisions for your life, and all who wait for Him will be blessed.

The Hebrew writer said,

> *That ye be not slothful, but followers of them who through faith and patience inherit the promises* (Hebrews 6:12).

The same writer wrote,

> *Cast not away therefore your confidence, which hath great recompence of reward. For ye have need of patience, that, after ye have done the will of God, ye might receive the promise* (Hebrews 10:35-36).

He encouraged us to recognize our need for patience, reminding us that it is through our faith and patience that our inheritance will be achieved.

Brother and sister, please don't give up. ***Please don't throw away your faith in those times that your faith is tested.*** Rejoice instead, because God loves you enough that He offers opportunities that develop your faith. He, at the same time, encourages you to understand that patience is something you need.

Patience is something that has a great effect upon your life and eternal soul, and through it comes that greatest of all rewards!

Chapter 50
Never Falling Again: God's Plan of Prevention

Godliness

What is Godliness? What does that word really mean?

When we look at any dictionary, the most common definitions seem to convey the idea of conforming to the wishes, desires, and commandments of God. It is a descriptor of deep devotion, and a desire to be as much like God as humanly possible. Jesus was "God in flesh." John 1:1 says,

> *In the beginning was the Word, and the Word was with God, and the Word was God.*

Follow down to v.14,

> *And the Word was made flesh, and dwelt among us, (and we beheld his glory, the glory as of the only begotten of the Father), full of grace and truth.*

Paul confirmed this in his first letter to Timothy. He wrote,

> *And without controversy great is the mystery of godliness: God was manifest in the flesh, justified in the Spirit, seen of angels, preached unto the Gentiles,*

> *believed on in the world, received up into*
> *glory* (1 Timothy 3:16).

How do we learn to be Godly, or to be like God? We learn to be like Jesus Christ – the Word that was made flesh and dwelt among us.

What was Jesus like? Jesus said,

> *Take my yoke upon you, and learn of me;*
> *for I am meek and lowly in heart: and ye*
> *shall find rest unto your souls* (Matthew
> 11:29).

Jesus Christ could have displayed a variety of personality types, but God in the flesh chose to be meek and lowly. This is where we begin. Throw off your arrogance and high-mindedness, because those attributes are not of the Lord and have no place in His body.

Hunger after righteousness. Jesus made a promise found in Matthew 5:6,

> *Blessed are they which do hunger and*
> *thirst after righteousness: for they shall be*
> *filled.*

If you will hunger after and pursue doing right, you will be filled and blessed.

Jesus was compassionate (Matthew 15:32), loving (Romans 5:8), prayerful (Luke 22:41-44), forgiving of others (Luke 23:34), a defender of God's will (Matthew 21:12), yet He was not violent to others (Matthew 26:52). Jesus didn't speak when He was falsely accused (Matthew 27:14). He served others (John 13:12-14), He spent time trying to teach those in sin (Matthew 9:10-13), He loved His enemies (Matthew 5:44), and He demonstrated a self-sacrificial love (John 15:13).

My puny and pitiful attempt to describe the Lord Jesus Christ does not begin to make a scratch in the description of His nature. My humble prayer is that this might simply help you to begin your own study of the wonderful Redeemer, and how you might begin to add Godliness to your patience.

Peter explains it far better than I,

> *Wherefore gird up the loins of your mind, be sober, and hope to the end for the grace that is to be brought unto you at the revelation of Jesus Christ; As obedient children, not fashioning yourselves according to the former lusts in your ignorance: But as he which hath called you*

is holy, so be ye holy in all manner of conversation [behavior]; Because it is written, Be ye holy; for I am holy (1 Peter 1:13-16).

How do you add patience to temperance (self-control)? Patience is a word that I have hated with a passion throughout my lifetime, but it is a learned skill that has given me a lifetime of the greatest and most valued of dividends.

To be patient is the self-imposed discipline to wait while enduring the never-ending voices shouting, *Now!* from the background of your soul. The act of willful patience is a battle within the mind.

If you are young, you need to read this section several times; however, if you're old, you already know the contents, and I doubt it will add a splinter to your knowledge of patience (but I thank you sincerely for your willingness to read this section).

It has been calculated that Jesus didn't begin His ministry until He was about 30 years old. This demonstrates patience. How? Jesus, the Son of God, the King of Kings and Lord of Lords, the Savior of the world, could have started His ministry at His discretion –

according to God's will, of course – at a much *earlier* age.

Compare this to our current world: we give our young the luxury of driving when they are a mere 16 years old. We allow our young men and women the opportunity to enlist into military service at the age of 18, and college students typically graduate at an average age of 23 (excluding any post-grad work). Yet, Jesus didn't begin His ministry until the age of 30?

Why didn't Jesus begin His ministry at 16, 18, or 23? While this question is rhetorical and we cannot know the answer, this might reveal a component of "patience" in God's equation.

There are a plethora of Scriptures that deal with and address the topic of patience, and I strongly encourage you to research and read each and every one of them.

Patience, according to our Father, is highly valued. Ecclesiastes 7:8 says,

> *Better is the end of a thing than the*
> *beginning thereof: and the patient in spirit*
> *is better than the proud in spirit.*

God admires those who diligently *demonstrate* patience. But how do we acquire patience? We don't. Yes, you read that right. We cannot acquire patience.

Patience, in spite of all of the contemporary suggestions (deep breathing, keep a list of the triggers that evoke our impatience, count to 10, etc.) is a skill that we cannot summon at our beck and call.

Patience is rather a *forced* behavior. Patience is exerted through a self-conscious force. We literally force ourselves to be calm and to wait. During times of distress and struggle, we must force ourselves, our minds, and our hearts to recognize that we control our anxiety.

How do we wrestle our anxiety and subdue it and replace anxiety with a state of waiting calm? We remind ourselves of the *location* of our one true trust. *This* is the one thing that we *can* do.

Where does our trust reside? Is our trust in our individual control? Is our trust in our bank account? Is our trust in another human being? Is our trust in our job? Is our trust in our identity or self-image? Is our trust in our assets, our cash, or our land? Or is the location of our trust in the God of Heaven? We must continually remind ourselves of the *location* of our trust – we trust *in God*.

Here is an immutable fact: God is too good to be cruel and He is too wise to make a mistake; therefore, you can trust Him with your life, your life on earth, and your life in that eternal spectrum.

Chapter 51
Never Falling Again:
God's Plan of Prevention

Brotherly Kindness

Kindness is critical to your soul, but it is equally as important due to its effect on your brethren, the church.

It is sad that you and I have run into a few mean, unkind brethren. However, we must remember that the church is composed of humans who are weak, flawed, and sinful. This is, in and of itself, another test of our faith.

Proverbs 16:24 says,

> *Pleasant words are as an honeycomb,*
> *sweet to the soul, and health to the bones.*

Kindness goes hand-in-hand with encouragement, and the power of kindness (or unkindness) is immeasurable in its effect and reach.

Peter doesn't use the word *kindness* by itself, but says that we are to add *brotherly* kindness to Godliness. This type of kindness conveys a deep love for your brother and sister in Christ – the type of love that goes beyond a feeling or a nice greeting. It is, rather, a kindness that moves us toward developing a servant's heart.

Brotherly kindness is a litmus test for a true Christian. John said,

> *He that saith he is in the light, and hateth*
> *his brother, is in darkness even until now.*

*He that loveth his brother abideth in the
light, and there is none occasion of
stumbling in him* (1 John 2:9-10).

We are reminded of the need of brotherly kindness throughout the Word. Peter mentions it several times (1 Peter 1:22; 2:17; 3:8).

Consider how this issue is addressed in Leviticus,

*Thou shalt not go up and down as a
talebearer among thy people: neither shalt
thou stand against the blood of thy
neighbour: I am the LORD. Thou shalt not
hate thy brother in thine heart: thou shalt
in any wise rebuke thy neighbour, and not
suffer sin upon him* (19:16-17).

Chapter 52
Never Falling Again: God's Plan of Prevention

Charity (Love)

The word *charity* in this context means *love*. Add to brotherly kindness *love*. It is agape love (*agápē* from the Modern Greek).

This type of love encompasses a love for all mankind. God loves every soul (John 3:16). He loves your enemy; therefore, how can you hate a one whom God loves?

Jesus commands us all to love our enemies,

> *Ye have heard that it hath been said, Thou shalt love thy neighbour, and hate thine enemy.*
>
> *But I say unto you, Love your enemies, bless them that curse you, do good to them that hate you, and pray for them which despitefully use you, and persecute you; That ye may be the children of your Father which is in heaven: for he maketh his sun to rise on the evil and on the good, and sendeth rain on the just and on the unjust.*
>
> *For if ye love them which love you, what reward have ye? do not even the publicans*

the same? And if ye salute your brethren
only, what do ye more than others? do not
even the publicans so? Be ye therefore
perfect, even as your Father which is in
heaven is perfect (Matthew 5:43-48).

Love your enemies. Do good to them that hate you.
Pray for them that use and persecute you. Why? So that
we may be the children of God.

This type of love would cure the world of most of its
problems. Think about this: if everyone loved one
another with this type of love, there would be no crime,
no wars, and no poverty. There would be no militaries,
no judicial system, no lawyers, or police officers.

The Holy Spirit, through Paul's hand, penned some
of the most beautiful words describing this kind of love,

Though I speak with the tongues of men
and of angels, and have not charity, I am
become as sounding brass, or a tinkling
cymbal. And though I have the gift of
prophecy, and understand all mysteries,
and all knowledge; and though I have all
faith, so that I could remove mountains,
and have not charity, I am nothing. And

though I bestow all my goods to feed the poor, and though I give my body to be burned, and have not charity, it profiteth me nothing.

Charity [love] *suffereth long, and is kind; charity envieth not; charity vaunteth not itself, is not puffed up, Doth not behave itself unseemly, seeketh not her own, is not easily provoked, thinketh no evil; Rejoiceth not in iniquity, but rejoiceth in the truth;*

Beareth all things, believeth all things, hopeth all things, endureth all things. Charity never faileth: but whether there be prophecies, they shall fail; whether there be tongues, they shall cease; whether there be knowledge, it shall vanish away.

For we know in part, and we prophesy in part. But when that which is perfect is come, then that which is in part shall be done away. When I was a child, I spake as a child, I understood as a child, I thought as a child: but when I became a man, I put away childish things.

For now we see through a glass, darkly; but then face to face: now I know in part; but then shall I know even as also I am known.

And now abideth faith, hope, charity, these three; but the greatest of these is charity (1 Corinthians 13:1-13).

The greatest of these is **love**.

Brother and sister, you *can* come back to God. You can live life in the forgiveness, love, mercy, and grace of God. There's only one thing that stands in your way... *your* "John."

From the mire and vomit to forgiveness and restoration. Can you come from where you are at this moment or where you have been, to become a Christian who bears fruit? Can God use you?

Of course He can!

Brother and sister, please give this your most serious consideration. Your eternal soul depends on your decision.

Jonetta and I pray for you. I am confident that God will work on your heart and that you will make the best decision of your life... coming back to the Lord Jesus Christ and His bride, the church.

We pray for you and send to you our sincere Christian love.

ORDERING INFORMATION

Buy single or multiple copies on sale. We also offer deep discounts for multiple copies direct from the author at:

michaelshankministries.com

Find us on Facebook at:

https://www.facebook.com/pages/Muscle-and-a-Shovel/225178630892427

You can also order from Amazon.com, Barnes & Noble, Books-a-Million, Ingram Books, The Book Depository, and many Christian bookstores across the nation.

OTHER PUBLICATIONS
Muscle and a Shovel
Muscle and a Shovel eBook (*Kindle, Amazon.com, iTunes*)
Muscle and a Shovel 13-Week Student Workbook
Muscle and a Shovel 13-Week Teacher's Manual
Muscle and a Shovel Spanish Version
Muscle and a Shovel Portuguese Version
Muscle and a Shovel Audio Book

When Shovels Break
When Shovels Break (*Kindle, Amazon.com, iTunes*)

Revel Knox: Seven Times From Hell (*western novel with the gospel and the plan of salvation embedded within the story*)
Revel Knox: 7 Times from Hell eBook (*Kindle, Amazon.com, iTunes*)

Muscle and a Shovel FREE Online Periodical Newsletter (*features Inspirational conversion stories and pictures*)

Story Photos

Our home in Lake Dallas, Texas, where a large part of this story took place (2004).

Our one hundred-year-old farmhouse (photo August 2014). Rural Massac County, Illinois.

"John" when he was using steroids (Chapter 11, p.89).

Michael during his electrical contracting business (Chapter 29, p.223).

Michael and Jonetta Shank shortly after moving into the parsonage in Metropolis, Illinois (Chapter 34, p.263).

Michael Shank, photographed outside of the parsonage prior to first sermon at Metropolis, Illinois, Nov. 2, 2008.

Michael "John" Shank
in the pulpit (2014).

Isn't it an amazing fact that God can take a horrible, wretched, filthy rag and wash it clean? God *can* clean you up and make you *useful* for the kingdom of Jesus Christ! To God be *all* the honor, credit, glory and praise!

Friend, God has a plan for *you*. I am living proof. Therefore, I beg that you not give up. Prodigal, won't you come back? God is waiting to welcome you with open arms of love and forgiveness.

I Am Your Brother with Sincere Love,

Michael Shank

Scripture References

Preface
Mark 2:17

Chapter 3
James 1:14-15

Chapter 5
Mark 4:13-20

Chapter 6
Philippians 4:4-7

Chapter 8
Matthew 5:45

Chapter 10
1 Corinthians 3:1
James 4:13-15
Acts 10: 34-35
Deuteronomy 31:6
Romans 5:8
1 John 4:10
Titus 2:11-12
John 1:17
John 1:1-4
Acts 20:52

Chapter 11
Proverbs 16:18

Chapter 14
2 Samuel 12:13
1 John 1:8-9
Hebrews 4:12
Colossians 2:11-13

Chapter 15
2 Samuel 11:7-27
2 Corinthians 10:12
Job 7:6

Chapter 16
Revelation 2:10
Revelation 2:4-5
James 5:16
1 John 1:1-9
John 4:10
John 4:14
1 Peter 2:2
John 6:33
Hebrews 5:12

Psalm 119:103
Matthew 12:43-45
2 Peter 2:20-22

Chapter 18
Deuteronomy 30:19-20
Luke 15:11-32
2 Peter 3:9
Matthew 9:11-13

Chapter 19
Romans 5:7

Chapter 20
John 4:21-23
Luke 15:10

Chapter 21
Jeremiah 29:11
Acts 20:28
Acts 9:3-6
Acts 9:17-18
Acts 22:12-16
John 5:3-9

Chapter 23
James 1:27

Chapter 24
Mark 10:2-12
Acts 4:12
Matthew 19:24
Matthew 5:8
1 Corinthians 1:10

Chapter 26
John 17:20-21
Colossians 1:18
Ephesians 4:4
1 Peter 3:21
Acts 20:7
Ephesians 5:19

Chapter 28
Luke 3:8
Ephesians 1:7-8
1 John 1:4-10
Jeremiah 29:11-13
Hebrews 8:12

Chapter 29
Luke 12:48
2 Corinthians 5:10
Matthew 6:14-15

Chapter 33
Ephesians 3:20

Chapter 35
Ephesians 3:20
1 Corinthians 1:29

Chapter 37
John 14:15
John 2:3
1 John 5:3
Matthew 22:36-40
1 Corinthians 13:13
Matthew 18:15
Proverbs 20:19
2 Timothy 3:1-5
1 Timothy 5:12-13
1 Peter 4:15
1 Timothy 5:12-13
1 Peter 4:15
2 Thessalonians 3:11-12

Chapter 38
Philippians 3:13
Mark 2:16-17
Acts 3:19
Acts 8:37
Acts 2:38
Romans 6:3-6
Acts 2:47
Psalm 119:105
1 John 1:7
Revelation 2:10
Luke 15:18-19
1 John 1:7
1 John 1:9
James 5:16
John 1:7-9
Titus 1:2
Matthew 5:43-45
Romans 8:7
Romans 5:8-11
Hebrews 4:15
John 8:1-11
Acts 2
Romans 6:1-2
1 Thessalonians 4:7
2 Timothy 1:9
1 Peter 1:13-16

1 John 2:1
Isaiah 55:7

Chapter 39
Revelation 21:8
Matthew 18:23-35
Matthew 18:21

Chapter 40
Matthew 7:7-8
James 5:17-18
1 Peter 1:20-21
2 Corinthians 1:13

Chapter 40 cont.
1 Corinthians 14:33
Ephesians 3:3-5
Matthew 26:36-44
Isaiah 55:8
1 John 5:13-14
Matthew 6:8
Philippians 4:19
Colossians 1:16-17

Chapter 41
1 Corinthians 1:7-8
2 Corinthians 1:7-11
1 Corinthians 12:8-13
Jonah 1-2

Chapter 42
Genesis 2:18
Genesis 1:26
Mark 6:7
1 Samuel 18:1
Ecclesiastes 4:9-12
1 Corinthians 15:33
John 15:33

Chapter 43
1 Corinthians 15:13-19
1 Corinthians 15:1-6
1 Corinthians 15:9-10
Ephesians 2:4-8
Romans 3:23
1 John 1:8-10
Romans 6:3-5
Galatians 3:26-27
Ephesians 2:5
Ephesians 1:3

Chapter 44
Revelation 2:10
2 Peter 1:10-11

Chapter 45
2 Peter 1:10-11
2 Peter 1:5-7
2 Peter 1:8
2 Peter 1:9
Isaiah 55:11

Chapter 46
Proverb 3:1-3
Philippians 4:7-8
Proverb 23:7
Matthew 15:17-20

Chapter 47
Hosea 4:6
2 Corinthians 2:11
Jeremiah 10:23
John 17:17
Psalm 109:115
2 Timothy 3:16-17
Proverb 19:2
Romans 10:1-3

Chapter 48
Romans 7:15-20
Philippians 3:13-14
Romans 13:14
1 Corinthians 9:27
Matthew 4:1-11
Matthew 26:41

Chapter 49
Psalm 62:1
James 1:4
James 1:2-3
Psalm 46:10
Psalm 130:5-6
Isaiah 30:18
Hebrews 6:12
Hebrews 10:35-36

Chapter 50
John 1:1
John 1:1-4
1 Timothy 3:16
Matthew 11:29
Matthew 5:6
Matthew 15:32
Romans 5:8
Luke 22:41-44
Luke 23:34
Matthew 21:12
Matthew 26:52

Matthew 27:14
John 13:12-14
Matthew 9:10-13
Matthew 5:4
John 15:13
1 Peter 1:13-16
Ecclesiastes 7:8

Chapter 51
Proverb 16:24
1 John 2:9-10
1 Peter 1:22
1 Peter 2:17
1 Peter 3:8
Leviticus 19:16-17

CPSIA information can be obtained
at www.ICGtesting.com
Printed in the USA
BVOW04s1954041116

466710BV00010B/53/P